Heaven on Earth

Sejal Macwan

English Translation by Shefali Dass
Edited by Preeti Gurjar and Shefali Dass

New Harbor Press
RAPID CITY, SD

Copyright © 2022 by Sejal Macwan.

All rights reserved. No part of this publication may be reproduced, distributed or transmitted in any form or by any means, including photocopying, recording, or other electronic or mechanical methods, without the prior written permission of the publisher, except in the case of brief quotations embodied in critical reviews and certain other noncommercial uses permitted by copyright law. For permission requests, write to the publisher, addressed "Attention: Permissions Coordinator," at the address below.

Macwan/New Harbor Press
1601 Mt.Rushmore Rd, Ste 3288
Rapid City, SD 57701
www.newharborpress.com

Cover and logo design by Tim's Dezine & Embroidery
Email : timdezine@gmail.com

Ordering Information:
Quantity sales. Special discounts are available on quantity purchases by corporations, associations, and others. For details, contact the "Special Sales Department" at the address above.

Heaven on Earth/ Sejal Macwan. —1st ed.
ISBN 978-1-63357-434-2

Table of Contents

I. INTRODUCTION
1. Book Dream 1

II. BOOK EXPLANATION
2. Explanation Book Dream 3
3. Data Entry Job Dream 4

III. LIFE OF MANKIND
4. Earth's Life Span 5
5. God's Glory 6
6. God's Commandment 6
7. Creation of the Woman 8
8. Woman's Husband 8
9. The Woman—Weaker Vessel 9
10. Adam—Likeness of Who Was to Come 10
11. New Beginning 11
12. Woman's Seed 12
13. Adulterous Woman 12
14. Death of Woman's Husband 13
15. Woman's Hair for Covering 14
16. Chaste Virgin 15
17. Virgin Shall Bear a Son 16

18. Who Are Israelites?..17

19. Tares for Purification 17

20. God Blessed Ishmael for Our Purification....................19

21. Physical and Spiritual Body...................................22

22. Son of Man..24

23. Baptism of Jesus..25

24. Joseph's Dream...26

25. Parable of Resurrection.......................................27

IV. SPIRITUAL LIFE

26. Tree 29

27. Fig Tree 30

28. Fig Tree Cursed..31

29. Soul..31

30. Prophet...34

31. Temple 36

32. Deep Waters..40

33. Baptism of the Holy Spirit 43

34. Thief...45

35. Tithes 47

36. Two Witnesses...48

37. Burden Carrier 55

V. THE SON OF MAN

38. Firstborn...57

39. Knowing God 61

40. Rod of Iron 62

41. Son of David 66

42. Son 67

43. Gift of God 70

44. Blood of Jesus 71

45. Jesus' Coming Leading to Life 73

46. Shefali's Coming of Christ 82

47. Jesus' Coming in My (Sejal's) Life 82

48. Jesus' Coming Leading to Death 83

49. Lamentations of God 86

50. Life of Mankind 88

VI. NATION OF ISRAEL

51. Ground (Land) 93

52. Earth Is Hell 102

53. Belly 105

54. Garden of Eden 108

55. Wrath of God 110

56. Seed of a Woman 112

57. Adam's Helper 114

58. White Dove's Vision 115

59. New Creation 116

60. Sabbath Day 118

VII. ANGEL

61. The Sign of Abomination 123

62. Jesus Fully Revealed God 125

63. Face of God 129

64. Angel 130

65. Lucifer 136

66. Victory 141

67. Pool of Siloam 143

VIII. LIFE ON EARTH

68. Sin 145

69. Image of God 146

70. God's Image Is Man and Woman 150

71. Sacrifice 158

72. Asked for a Son 161

73. Journey 163

74. Love of Jesus 164

75. Yoke 166

76. Debt 167

77. Rich 167

78. Meaning of Parables 171

79. Woman—Physical Body 173

80. Do Not Empower the Devil 176

81. Second Death 178

82. Esau 180

83. Cain 181

IX. FORMS OF JESUS

84. Abel 183

85. Job 183

86. Abraham 184

87. Joseph 185

88. Ruben 186

89. City of Refuge 186

90. Moses 187

91. Jephthah 188

92. Barak 188

93. David 189

94. Solomon 194

95. Ahab 195

96. Nebuchadnezzar 195

97. Daniel 197

98. Tamar 197

99. Korah 198

100. Adam—Beginning of God's Creation 199

101. God Gave Birth to the Son 200

102. Adam - Son of God 202

103. Gentile (Adulterous Woman) 206

X. DREAMS

104. God's Kingdom Inside of Me (Sejal) 209

105. Samson Tore the Lion Apart Dream 210

106. Daniel's Den of Lions Dream 210

107. Heaven on Earth 211

108. Pregnancy Dream 211

109. Husband's House 212
110. Mirror Dream 213

ONE

Introduction

1. Book Dream

In the year 2000, I accepted Jesus Christ as my Lord and Savior. During those days, I was fasting and praying a lot. At that time, I was thinking if Jesus comes to visit me, I would never let him go as Jacob wrestled with God and didn't let Him go. In those days, I had a dream where Jesus appeared to me in His glory. I ran after Him to catch Him, but I fell on my face in the dirt and I heard a voice saying, "Get up." I looked up and saw a glorified angel. He was wearing a white shiny gown. The color of his hair was silver, and he had two large white wings. He said, "God the Father has sent a book for you." I saw a basket in his hand, made of wood splints, holding two books within it—*Praktikaran* written on one in Gujarati and *Revelation* written on the other. I took the one that had Gujarati writing, then my dream ended. God asked me to write this book in 2021 and this is that book.

TWO

Book Explanation

2. Explanation Book Dream

When God the Father showed me in a dream to write this book, I saw that I was sitting in a room of the lowest floor of a very high-rise building. After that, in the same building, there was a stairwell and I started climbing up. In a very short time, I was on the roof of the building. I looked down from the roof of the building and the building was so high that I could see the whole Earth. There were many other buildings around the building I was on, but they were all smaller compared to the building I was on. The building I was on was the highest building among others. Then, I lifted my hands high and I started flying, as if I could reach any place in a moment. There were four angels who were standing and waiting for me. They had armor and swords like soldiers. Those four angels had large white wings. We were walking together, with two soldiers in front of me and two behind. Then, the two large hands of God the Father stopped me. God the Father had one hand on my shoulder and one hand was on my chest and said, "Would you write a book about me?" I told God the Father, "Yes, I would." I thought to myself, "What kind of book?" He stated right away, "An explanation book." After that, the hands of God the Father left, and we walked farther and reached a place where a pond was. The water in that pond was black like asphalt and immediately it turned bright purple. That light was very bright, then my dream ended.

This book explains how God is and what kind of love He has for us.

3. Data Entry Job Dream

The job I currently have is not a permanent job. After every twelve months of work, they give us a leave for three months. After the three months leave is completed, the employer hires us back. God talked to me through a dream about writing this book. In my dream, I was sitting down, and I heard God the Father's voice saying to me, "Daughter, when you are on your three months leave, I will give you a data entry job." I told Him, "Those days are my days to stay home, and will I have to work? I will only do part-time data entry job," then my dream ended. In the morning, when I woke up and remembered that dream, I realized the meaning of it. Moses had received a data entry job to write the first five books and, in the same way, God has given me this data entry job. God the Father would speak and explain, and I would write the book. This is the way I have written this book.

THREE

Life of Mankind

4. Earth's Life Span

In the beginning, God created the heavens and the Earth and on the seventh day God ended His work. Paul said, "Although the works were finished from the foundation of the world. For He has spoken in a certain place of the seventh day in this way: 'And God rested on the seventh day from all His works'" (Hebrews 4:3–4). David said, "The days of our lives are seventy years; and if by reason of strength they are eighty years" (Psalm 90:10).

The life span of the Earth is 7,000 years and by reason of strength, they are 8,000 years. David said, "So teach us to number our days, that we may gain a heart of wisdom" (Psalm 90:12). "Beloved, do not forget this one thing, that with the Lord one day is as a thousand years, and a thousand years as one day" (2 Peter 3:8).

Thus, the days of creation are seven which means the life span of the Earth is 7,000 years. The life span of the Earth is 7,000 years and the day of resurrection will be on eighth day in fourth millennium AD (years 7001–8000). Behold the new Heaven and new Earth, we are new creation in Christ Jesus. Old things have passed away; behold, all things have become new. Be transformed by the renewing of your mind and receive the eternal heritage.

5. God's Glory

God created mankind from dust. He created them male and female. In the image of God, male and female. The Lord God formed man of the dust of the ground and breathed into his nostrils the breath of life, and man became a living being. In God was life, and the life was the light of men.

God lived inside of Adam and Eve, and they were experiencing the glory of God with Him. God is light and in Him was life. Jesus said that if your eye is good, your whole body will be full of light. That is the glory of God. They lived with God, experiencing the glory of God—death had no power on them. They had life within them; they had no need to wear clothes as their bodies were full of light and God's glory. Adam and Eve were naked, but they were not ashamed.

Thus, God is light and life itself and, within Him, there is no darkness or death—both have no power over Him.

As the Scripture says, the gates of Hades (death) shall not prevail against the church. As we are a temple of the Living God, full of His glory, the same way as Adam and Eve were when God lived inside of them.

6. God's Commandment

God's commandment was to not eat the fruit of the tree of the knowledge of good and evil because, on the day you eat of it, you will surely die. But Eve ate the fruit, gave it to Adam, and he ate. Thus, they broke God's commandment and death came as God had told them. God left from inside of them. The power of darkness came upon them, and death reigned in them.

Jesus said, "If therefore the light that is in you is darkness, how great is that darkness!" Adam said, "I was naked, so I hid myself." Scripture says that everyone is naked and exposed in hell. God left, life left, light left, and we became blind relative to God. Jesus said that if the blind leads the blind, they both will fall into a ditch. No one has seen God because we are in darkness, hell, and suffering pain, all because we disobeyed and broke our relationship with God, separated from Him.

The way Jesus said, "My God, My God, why have you forsaken me?" Jesus took all our sins, and upon becoming sinful, God left him, meaning life and light itself left Jesus, allowing death and darkness to come.

Jesus is the express image of God (His person). As Jesus said that you abide in Me, and I in you. By this, My Father is glorified that you bear much fruit. If you abide in Me, and My words abide in you.

Thus, if we abide in Jesus and He in us, by this, God abides in us. Adam and Eve were experiencing the same glory of God in the Garden of Eden. God lived inside of them, and they lived inside of God, and they were one with God in spirit as Jesus said, "My Father and I are one."

But Eve (woman), by eating the forbidden fruit that is sin, joined together with the lust of the flesh, was separated from God and became carnal. By sinning, the woman was separated from God the Father and the relationship between them was broken because God is holy and not carnal and does not sin. Thus, God departed from her, and the death and darkness came on the woman.

When a voice came from heaven saying that I have both glorified it and will glorify it again, "Jesus answered and said, This voice came not because of me, but for your sakes. Now is the judgment of this world: now shall the prince of this world be cast out. And I, if I be lifted up from the Earth, will draw all men unto me" (John 12:30–32 KJV). Thus, we will be glorified again, the way we were in glory with God in the Garden of Eden, in the same way we will be glorified again in the kingdom of God.

7. Creation of the Woman

"The LORD God formed man of the dust of the ground, and breathed into his nostrils the breath of life; and man became a living soul." (Genesis 2:7)

Adam means "Earth" in the Hebrew language. We were all created from just one man, Adam. This is how we are all children of Adam.

And the Lord God said, "It is not good that man should be alone; I will make him a helper comparable to him" (Genesis 2:18). "But for Adam there was not found a helper comparable to him" (Genesis 2:20).

"For when God made a promise to Abraham, because He could swear by no one greater, He swore by Himself" (Hebrews 6:13). In the same way, the helper who is comparable to Adam was searched and could not be found. "And the LORD God caused a deep sleep to fall on Adam, and he slept; and He took one of his ribs and closed up the flesh in its place. Then the rib which the LORD God had taken from man He made into a woman, and He brought her to the man" (Genesis 2:21–22). And Adam said: "This is now bone of my bones and flesh of my flesh; She shall be called Woman, because she was taken out of Man" (Genesis 2:23). This is how woman was created.

8. Woman's Husband

"The LORD God commanded the man, saying, 'Of every tree of the garden you may freely eat; but of the tree of the knowledge of good and evil you shall not eat, for in the day that you eat of it you shall surely die'" (Genesis 2:16–17). But the serpent deceived the woman, and she took the fruit and ate, listening to the devil and consequently became subjected to the devil and sinned. By disobeying, she experienced sin and gave the devil authority over herself. "The Lord said to Cain, 'Why are you angry? And why has your countenance fallen? If you do well, will you not be accepted? And if you do not do well, sin lies at the door. And its desire is for you, but you should rule over it" (Genesis 4:6–7). Instead of ruling over sin, we will become slave to sin if we give in to sin. Woman sinned and made the devil her husband and ruler and gave authority to the devil.

First commandment is "You shall have no other gods," but the woman listened to the devil and broke God's commandment. Second is "You shall not bow down to idols nor serve them," but she served the devil. Third is "You shall not take the name of the LORD your God in vain," but she sinned and tested God. These ways, woman disobeyed and rebelled against God.

9. The Woman—Weaker Vessel

The woman ate the fruit of the tree of the knowledge of good and evil and, breaking God's commandment, experiencing sin, brought death upon herself as God had said that for in the day that you eat of it, you shall surely die.

Woman is a weak vessel who is weaker than man. Whatever was unseen, God has brought to seen and this is how we can see it.

Woman is all of mankind (all people on Earth) who have sinned and were subject to the devil. Scripture says, "For all have sinned and fall short of the glory of God" (Romans 3:23). "The head of woman is the man. Every woman who prays or prophesies with her head uncovered dishonors her head" (1 Corinthians 11:5). "For this reason, the woman ought to have a symbol of authority on her head" (1 Corinthians 11:10).

The Man is Jesus, who is head of the woman. And woman should be obedient to man, her husband who is Jesus, and obey all his commandments, and not disrespect her husband.

All the relationships that God has given us in this world, such as husband, wife, mother, father, brother, sister, friend, child, widow all are so we can understand God.

10. Adam—Likeness of Who Was to Come

"For Adam was formed first, then Eve and Adam was not deceived, but the woman being deceived, fell into transgression" (1 Timothy 2:13–14). Woman was deceived by the serpent (the devil) to eat the fruit of the tree of knowledge of good and evil.

"First Adam was a type of Him who was to come" (second Adam—Jesus) (Romans 5:14).

God made two great lights, the greater light to rule the day and the lesser light to rule the night. God created the sun, the moon, and the stars. God created sun on the fourth day as Jesus appeared on Earth in the Forth millennium (from the beginning of creation) and said I am the light of the world.

Jesus said to them, "Most assuredly, I say to you, before Abraham was, I AM" (John 8:58). "The men of Nineveh will rise up in the judgment with this generation and condemn it, because they repented at the preaching of Jonah; and indeed, a greater than Jonah is here" (Matthew 12:41).

This is how Adam was created first, then Eve. Eve took the fruit and ate and she also gave to her husband with her, and he ate as Jesus took our sins upon Himself on the cross and ate the fruit that woman gave Him. The gap between the woman eating the fruit and giving it to her husband is about 4,000 years.

When Adam ate the fruit, God said to Adam, "What is this you have done?" Cursed is the ground for your sake, meaning death came. God said, "In the sweat of your face, you shall eat bread" (Genesis 3:19), meaning you will have to work hard to earn the bread of life.

Jesus said, "Do not labor for the food which perishes, but for the food which endures to everlasting life, which the Son of Man will give you, because God the Father has set His seal on Him"

(John 6:27). In the Garden of Gethsemane, Jesus' sweat became like great drops of blood as God had said that in the sweat of your face, you shall get bread of life back, which Jesus did so for us by sacrificing His life. "It is expedient for us that one man should die for the people, and not that the whole nation (mankind) should perish" (John 11:50). We have redemption through His blood, the forgiveness of sins and by His stripes we are healed.

11. New Beginning

"To the woman He said: I will greatly multiply your sorrow and your conception; In pain you shall bring forth children; Your desire shall be for your husband, and he shall rule over you" (Genesis 3:16). By saying, "I will greatly multiply your sorrow and your conception," God means multiplying the pain in the process to bring forth a child, worsening the hardship in the process of a new beginning, sadness in repenting from sin, sorrow in new birth will greatly multiply.

Jesus said, "Most assuredly, I say to you, unless one is born again, he cannot see the kingdom of God" (John 3:3). Jesus said, behold, I make all things new. "Unless a grain of wheat falls into the ground and dies, it remains alone" (John 12:24) in the same way for a new beginning, to be born again, you will have suffering and will have to die to self. Paul said, "I labor in birth again until Christ is formed in you" (Galatians 4:19).

Scripture says, "We know that the whole creation groans and labors with birth pangs" (Romans 8:22). It labors with birth pangs for redemption the same way it's written for the woman (all mankind), "Nevertheless she will be saved in childbearing if they continue in faith, love, and holiness, with self-control" (1 Timothy 2:15). Thus, per the Scriptures, to have a new beginning we must be saved by giving birth to a divine Son (Christ formed in you), such as the Christ formed within ourselves upon accepting His Salvation.

12. Woman's Seed

The LORD God said to the serpent, "I will put enmity between you and the woman, and between your seed and her Seed; He shall bruise your head, and you shall bruise His heel" (Genesis 3:15).

Woman's seed means the second Adam (Jesus) who became life-giving spirit. When Jesus was tempted by the devil in the wilderness, being obedient to God, Jesus did not serve the devil (sin). By rejecting the devil, Jesus obeyed God's first commandment that "You shall have no other gods before me." When the devil said, "Fall down and worship me," Jesus didn't serve the devil but, instead, obeyed God's commandment that "You shall not bow down to idols nor serve them." When the devil asked Jesus to throw himself down from the pinnacle of the temple, by rejecting what the devil asked, Jesus didn't take the name of the Lord God in vain and didn't test God. This is how the first Adam disobeyed God's commandment and brought death on himself; but, the second Adam (Jesus), being obedient to God, never sinned and became life-giving spirit.

This is how God put enmity between woman and the serpent, serpent means sin. God put enmity between the woman's offspring that is born with new beginning, new birth and between the sin. So, woman's seed will crush the devil's (sin's) head.

13. Adulterous Woman

From the beginning, God created them man and a woman. But the woman sinned by disobeying God and eating the fruit of the tree of good and evil. She joined another husband, meaning she made the devil her second husband by sinning and gave the devil authority over herself. Thus, woman committed adultery. *Woman* means all the mankind. All of mankind who sinned and committed adultery and, by giving authority to the devil, worshipped the idol. Every sin that is against God is equal to idol worship.

Scripture says, "For all have sinned, and come short of the glory of God" (Romans 3:23 KJV).

The scribes and Pharisees brought to Jesus a woman caught in adultery. Now, Moses in the law commanded that such should be stoned. "For the wages of sin is death" (Romans 6:23). *Woman* means mankind, all the people on this Earth. Jesus said to the woman, "Neither do I condemn you; go and sin no more."

"For God did not send His Son into the world to condemn the world, but that the world through Him might be saved." (John 3:17)

14. Death of Woman's Husband

Paul writes that the woman who has a husband is bound by the law to her husband as long as he lives. But, if the husband dies, she is released from the law of her husband.

Woman's husband means the one who we give authority to by sinning. As long as that sin lives in us and we continue to sin, we are bound to the regulations of the law. The law is equal to stone and, with it, we destroy (kill) the sin as Jesus has said, "You judge according to the flesh," such as in the Old Testament, the adulterous woman was killed by stoning. There are many sins in our lives, and we kill them by the law. It's written not to bow down to idols and so, by not giving in to sin and by obeying the law, we bring death to sin.

"If her (woman's) husband dies, she is free from that law" (Romans 7:3). "The fruit of the Spirit is love, joy, peace, long-suffering, kindness, goodness, faithfulness, gentleness, self-control. Against such there is no law" (Galatians 5:22–23). These are a law to themselves. "Love is the fulfillment of the law" (Romans 13:10).

Scriptures says concerning virgins, "I have no commandment from the Lord. They are free from the law."

Woman's husband is the husband of sin (the devil), as long as he is alive, Paul says that woman is bound by the law; but, if "her husband dies," which means we destroy the works of the flesh by the Spirit, we (woman) become free from the law and against those there is no law.

The way Jesus took our sins upon Himself and gave His life on the cross, if we crucify our lust of the flesh (sin) on the cross and kill the husband of sin, we are no longer bound to the law, and we are free.

Paul says that I betrothed you to one husband, to present you as a pure virgin to Christ, who is without spot or wrinkle. As she who is married cares about the things of the world, the unmarried woman cares about the things of the Lord.

Scriptures say as the days of Noah were, so also will the coming of the Son of Man be. For, as in the days before the Flood, they were eating and drinking, marrying, and giving in marriage.

"For the desolate has many more children than she who has a husband" means the woman who has killed the husband of sin has more children than the one who is married.

The way a grain of wheat falls into the ground and dies, then bears fruits, in the same way when a husband dies, the woman, free from the law, gives many fruits. She will be fruitful, and God blesses her and says, "Go, be fruitful and multiply and fill the Earth."

The devil doesn't want you to be fruitful for God but that you stay barren and perish.

15. Woman's Hair for Covering

Woman has long hair for covering; but, if the woman has long hair, it is glory to her. With her hair, she can cover her nakedness.

Hair represents obedience. The man who is separated to serve the Lord keeps the vow of the Nazarene that no razor shall come upon his head.

For all the law is fulfilled in one word, *love*. Scripture says that *love* is fulfillment of the law and covers a multitude of sins.

If the woman prays or prophesies with *her head uncovered*, meaning she doesn't submit to Jesus, she *dishonors her head*, which means she dishonors Jesus as if *her head were shaved*, which means to be disobedient and rebellious as Eve was in the garden by eating the forbidden fruit.

16. Chaste Virgin

A chaste virgin is prepared to be presented to Christ as Paul says "that I may *present* you as a chaste virgin *to Christ*."

A *chaste virgin* is one who is betrothed to one husband. God gives that chaste virgin an opportunity to prove her love for Christ. The way when the daughter of Jephthah was going be offered up as burnt offering to God and she goes on a mountain to bewail her virginity. The mountain represents glory and, after that, she was offered up as burnt offering. In the same way, the chaste virgin also sacrifices her life for Christ. The way Jesus Christ dies and sacrifices His life, the chaste virgin also sacrifices her life. She sacrifices herself for Christ.

The way Esther did not consider her life dear, but put her life on the line to save the lives of God's people. The way Abraham offered up his only begotten son. The chaste virgin is given white fine linen to wear. Those are her righteous works. The chaste virgin is the one who learned the song of Moses and no one else could learn that song. The chaste virgin represents the 144,000 who are from the twelve tribes of Israel.

To become a chaste virgin from being a rebellious woman is a process. The way woman ate the fruit of the tree of the knowledge of good and evil and rebelled against God and by disobeying has her head shaved. After that, when woman grows her hair back by accepting Jesus Christ and obeying His commandments, she covers her head and honors her husband. She crucifies the flesh with its passions and desires and is free from the law. She becomes a widow and a virgin. Thus, she becomes the glorious church, without spot or wrinkle and without blemish for Christ, and demonstrates her love for Christ.

17. Virgin Shall Bear a Son

"Therefore the Lord himself shall give you a sign; Behold, a virgin shall conceive, and bear a son, and shall call his name Immanuel." (Isaiah 7:14 KJV)

According to the dream of Joseph, the sun represents the father, the moon represents the mother, and the stars, the brothers. The light of the sun shines on the moon. The moon does not have its own light, but the moon shines with the sun's light. This way, God the Father has given the law to Israel and the moon represents the people of Israel. By obeying the law, Israel kills the husband (the devil) of sin and becomes a chaste virgin. God's word says concerning virgins: "I have no commandment from the Lord—as they are law to themselves."

"The Holy Spirit will come upon you, and the power of the Highest will overshadow you; therefore, also, that Holy *One* who is to be born will be called the Son of God." (Luke 1:35)

Overshadow represents the obedience of the law (symbolized hair). God gave the law to Israel and the virgin bore a son which is the Christ. God said, "You are My Son, Today I have begotten You."

He will be great and will be called the Son of the Highest; and the Lord God will give Him the throne of His father David. And He will reign over the house of Jacob forever, and of His kingdom there will be no end. New heaven and new Earth, Jesus, said, "See I make all things new."

18. Who Are Israelites?

For he is not a Jew who is one outwardly but the one who also walks in the steps of the faith as Abraham had. (Romans 2 and 4)

Therefore, God gives His Holy Spirit to those who believe and the light of His law shines on them. The Holy Spirit overshadows them through the obedience of the law (symbolized hair), and they walk in the light and become chaste virgins and give birth to the Son. Blessed are those women through whom Christ appears and is born.

Scriptures say that Holy Spirit will come upon you and the power of the Highest will overshadow you and the one who is born will be called the son of God.

"Whoever has been born of God does not sin, for His seed remains in him; and he cannot sin, because he has been born of God." (1 John 3:9)

"For as many as are led by the Spirit of God, these are sons of God." (Romans 8:14)

19. Tares for Purification

Another parable He put forth to them, saying: "The kingdom of heaven is like a man who sowed good seed in his field; but while men slept, his enemy came and sowed tares among the wheat and went his way. But when the grain had sprouted and produced a crop, then the tares also appeared. So the servants of the owner came and said to him, 'Sir, did you not sow good seed in your field? How then does it have tares?' He said to them, 'An enemy has done this.' The servants said to him, 'Do you want us then to go and gather them up?' But he said, 'No, lest while you gather up the tares you also uproot the wheat with them. Let both grow together until the harvest, and at the time of harvest I will say to the reapers, 'First gather together the tares and bind them in bundles to burn them, but gather the wheat into my barn.'" (Matthew 13:24–30)

> The LORD God caused a deep sleep to fall on Adam, and he slept; and He took one of his ribs, and closed up the flesh in its place. Then the rib which the LORD God had taken from man He made into a woman, and He brought her to the man. (Genesis 2:21–22)

God caused a deep sleep to fall on Adam, meaning Jesus took our sins upon Himself and He gave us His glory and woman was redeemed by His blood. Thus, God created woman out of His ribs, woman is a weaker vessel. And Jesus reconciled us with God. Thus, God created woman out of Adam (Jesus).

To know how Abraham will get his inheritance, God asked Abraham to take a three-year-old heifer, a three-year-old female goat, and a three-year-old ram and cut them down in the middle. These three represent 3,000 years and the sacrifice on the altar represents Jesus who sacrificed His life for us. Now, when the sun was going down, a deep sleep fell upon Abraham; and, behold, horror and great darkness fell upon him. In the same way, when Jesus sacrificed His life on the cross, the sun was darkened for three hours. Jesus, who was innocent and guiltless, his enemy came and sowed tares in him. And it's written that, "When the vultures came down on the carcasses, Abraham drove them away" (Genesis 15:11). It's written also, "For wherever the carcass is, there the eagles will be gathered together" (Matthew 24:28).

Wherever death is, darkness is there and the wild birds gather together. The woman ate the fruit and gave it to her husband, and, upon eating it, all of mankind (woman) sinned, leading Jesus to carry that burden of sin on the cross. God told Abraham to know certainly that his descendants will be strangers in a land that is not theirs, and will serve them, and will be afflicted for 400 years. This means we were in bondage of sin for 4,000 years and, then, Jesus, the light of the world, came and freed us from the bondage of darkness (sin).

Cain killed Abel, now Abel represents Jesus and Cain represents the firstborn (body) flesh. It's written, "Therefore, whoever kills Cain, (meaning whoever kills the firstborn flesh) vengeance shall be taken on him sevenfold" (Genesis 4:15). This sevenfold vengeance means 7,000 vengeance shall be taken. This Earth is for 7,000 years only and after that circumcision on the eighth day means the everlasting covenant with God, there will be new Earth and new heaven. God said, "Behold, I make all things new" (Revelation 21:5).

Scriptures say, "A bruised reed He will not break, and smoking flax He will not quench, Till He sends forth justice to victory" (Matthew 12:20). God is saying that, until the bruised reed doesn't break and smoking flax doesn't quench, you (Jesus) sit at my right hand. God is saying that, until the death is swallowed up in victory, you sit at my right hand. Jesus is seated at the right hand of God until 7,000 years of the Earth is completed and Earth enters into 8,000 years in the fourth millennium AD. On that day, there will be a new heaven and a new Earth. Eighth day is the day of the resurrection and, on that day, Jesus and those who are to be firstfruits with Jesus will rise. On that day, death will be swallowed up in victory and Jesus will sit on the throne of His Father, the son of David will reign forever.

20. God Blessed Ishmael for Our Purification

Abraham had two sons: one with a bondwoman, born according to the flesh, and one with a free woman, born according to the Spirit. "But, as he who was born according to the flesh then persecuted him who was born according to the Spirit" (Galatians 4:29). Scriptures say, "God blessed Ishmael because he was also an offspring of Abraham. Ishmael was a hunter. I asked God, why did you bless Ishmael? He persecutes those who walk according to the Spirit. God answered, it's written, "Bless those who persecute you; bless and do not curse"

(Romans 12:14). When we bless and forgive those who persecute us, they grow more as we continue our walk with God.

> Peter says, Beloved, do not think it strange concerning the fiery trial which is to try you, as though some strange thing happened to you; but rejoice to the extent that you partake of Christ's sufferings, that when His glory is revealed, you may also be glad with exceeding joy. If you are reproached for the name of Christ, blessed are you, for the Spirit of glory and of God rests upon you. On their part He is blasphemed, but on your part He is glorified. (1 Peter 4:12–14)

This is how you are purified and love God more and more. Thus, for our purification, God blessed the tares.

> So the servants of the owner came and said to him, "Sir, did you not sow good seed in your field? How then does it have tares?" He said to them, "An enemy has done this." The servants said to him, "Do you want us then to go and gather them up?" But he said, "No, lest while you gather up the tares you also uproot the wheat with them. Let both grow together until the harvest, and at the time of harvest I will say to the reapers, 'First gather together the tares and bind them in bundles to burn them, but gather the wheat into my barn.'" (Matthew 13:27–30)

The ones born according to the flesh that has flesh and blood will not inherit the kingdom of God. They will perish, but the ones born of the Spirit who walk by the Spirit are the ones who came through good seed, and they will be *gathered in God's barn*, meaning they will enter the kingdom of God.

Tares (weed) represent our physical body which lusts after fleshly desires and sins. God blessed that physical body that it should last for 7,000 years. Because the Scriptures say, that is also a descendant of Abraham. The life of this Earth is 7,000 years and the life of mankind is also 7,000 years. If we remove the tares (weed) from ourselves, which is the lust of the flesh, we have eternal life through Jesus Christ. As Jesus said, that I have come that they may have life, and that they may have it more abundantly. That life will never end; Jesus gives life that never fades away. So, we are not one, but we are two, physical and spiritual. If we live by the flesh, we will perish; but, if we live by the Spirit, we have eternal life.

> Therefore, He said: "A certain nobleman went into a far country to receive for himself a kingdom and to return. So, he called ten of his servants, delivered to them ten minas, and said to them, 'Do business till I come.' But his citizens hated him, and sent a delegation after him, saying, 'We will not have this man to reign over us.' And so it was that when he returned, having received the kingdom, he then commanded these servants, to whom he had given the money, to be called to him, that he might know how much every man had gained by trading. Then came the first, saying, 'Master, your mina has earned ten minas.' And he said to him, 'Well done, good servant; because you were faithful in a very little, have authority over ten cities.' And the second came, saying, 'Master, your mina has earned five minas.' Likewise, he said to him, 'You also be over five cities.' Then another came, saying, 'Master, here is your mina, which I have kept put away in a handkerchief. For I feared you, because you are an austere man. You collect what you did not deposit, and reap what you did not sow.' And he said to him, 'Out of your own mouth I will judge you, you wicked servant. You knew that I was an austere man, collecting what I did not deposit and reaping what I did not sow. Why then did you not put my money in the bank, that at my coming I might have collected it with interest?'" (Luke 19:12–23)

The enemy sowed the tares, but God used them for our good. Every branch that bears fruit He prunes, that it may bear more fruit.

This is how our God reaps where He did not sow—He didn't sow tares, but He uses them for our purification to change our lives. Therefore, all things work together for good in Christ.

21. Physical and Spiritual Body

We are not one but two, a physical body and spiritual body. As it is written in the Scriptures, Abraham had two sons: one from a bondwoman who is under bondage and one from a free woman who is through promise by his wife. Ishmael, who is a son of a bondwoman, is under the bondage of sin and is slave to sin. Therefore, Sarah said to Abraham, "Cast out this bondwoman and her son: for the son of this bondwoman shall not be heir with my son, even with Isaac" (Genesis 21:10 KJV).

As the Scriptures say, "Flesh and blood cannot inherit the kingdom of God" (1 Corinthians 15:50). Physical body (flesh) lusts after sin. If we by the lust of the flesh become slave to sin, we will surely die, but if we live by the Spirit and destroy the works of the flesh, we will have eternal life and inherit God's kingdom. *Death* means separation from God for eternity, but, if we walk by the Spirit faithfully, we are heirs of God and God is our inheritance. This is the way Isaac, who represents spiritual body, received the inheritance.

"(For the children being not yet born, neither having done any good or evil, that the purpose of God according to election might stand, not of works, but of him that calleth;) it was said unto her, The elder shall serve the younger. As it is written, Jacob have I loved, but Esau have I hated." (Romans 9:11–13 KJV)

First is the physical body (flesh, Esau) and the second is the spiritual body (Jacob). So, the older, which is the flesh, will serve the spiritual, which is the younger. We should not become slave to sin but rule over the sin.

Esau came in from the field, and he was weary, he sold his birthright to Jacob for some red stew and despised his birthright. Esau represents Jesus. "Looking unto Jesus, the author and finisher of our faith, who for the joy that was set before

Him endured the cross, despising the shame, and has sat down at the right hand of the throne of God" (Hebrews 12:2).

Jesus shed his blood to save us and suffered death for us. When Jesus took our sins on Himself, God left Him, and death came upon him. Jesus said, "My God, My God, why have you forsaken me?" When death came upon Jesus, He went into the deep darkness and, as in the Sheol, everyone is naked and uncovered, He became naked and God asked, "Adam, Adam where are you?" Then, Adam said, "I was naked; and I hid myself." This is how Jesus sowed his physical body for us and sacrificed himself.

King David had two sons with Bathsheba. When the firstborn became sick, David prayed to God for seven days, but God told David that the child of fornication shall surely die, thus, the child died. This first child represents the physical body (flesh), and it will be for 7,000 years only. After that, it will be destroyed and the eighth day (fourth millennium AD) is the day of resurrection. Scriptures say, heaven and Earth will pass away, and God will make new heaven and new Earth, therefore, will make all things new. This is how the physical body is sowed and the spiritual body is raised. Visible things will go away and only the invisible will last. The unseen will last forever. Now, what is becoming obsolete and growing old is ready to vanish away. What is seen is temporary. As for man, his days are like grass, here today and gone tomorrow, but God is forever.

David's second son, Solomon—God named him *Jedidiah*, meaning beloved of Yahweh and son of David—will reign forever who is spiritual.

Jesus is not one but two: spiritual and physical. When Jesus came from Galilee to John at the Jordan to be baptized by him, John said to Jesus that I need to be baptized by You, and are You coming to me? But Jesus answered and said to him to permit it to be so now, for thus it is fitting for us to fulfill all righteousness. Then, he allowed Him. Jesus had never sinned, but He took our sins upon Himself and, by sacrificing His flesh, He brought death on Himself. Thus, Jesus sacrificed Himself and gave up His physical body for our sins the way wheat is sowed in the ground and took baptism.

Baptism means to bury our sinful flesh and giving up sin, live by the Spirit and die to sin. It means to be born again and have a new beginning. God says that He makes all things new.

Abraham was going to sacrifice Isaac, his only begotten son, concluding that God was able to raise him up, even from the dead.

When Abraham went to sacrifice Isaac, his promised son (represents Jesus), Scriptures say Abraham saw the place afar off: the place was three days journey, meaning 3,000 years afar. According to the Parable of the Resurrection, he also received him back. The promise of resurrection that God gave was on the fourth day, meaning in the fourth millennium AD, God will raise from the dead and the dead will rise first.

"Your father Abraham rejoiced to see My day, and he saw it and was glad" (John 8:56). Abraham saw that physical body is sowed and spiritual body is raised. Jesus said, *God is* the God of Abraham, the God of Isaac, and the God of Jacob. He is not the God of the dead, but the God of the living. They had life in them, and God was in them, and they were one with God.

Those who are slaves to sin are dead relative to God and God is not inside of them.

22. Son of Man

Son of man Jesus is a man Himself. The first Adam lost his *place* (status) by eating the fruit of the tree of knowledge of good and evil. To restore that status, the son of God, Jesus, was born on this Earth as a son of man through a virgin. He came to restore all from where Adam had fallen. First Adam sinned by disobeying, but the second Adam (Jesus) obeyed in all things.

Scriptures say, "Who, being in the form of God, did not consider it robbery to be equal with God" (Philippians 2:6). Jesus had glory in heaven with God as Moses had glory in the palace. Moses rejected to be called the son of the Pharaoh's sister but instead freed his brethren from slavery. In the same way, Jesus left all His glory and came on this Earth. Scriptures say, "He made Himself of no reputation, taking the form of a bondservant, and coming in the likeness of men. And being found in appearance as a man, He humbled Himself and became obedient to the point of death, even the death of the cross" (Philippians 2:7–8). "Though He was a Son, yet He learned obedience by the things which He suffered" (Hebrews 5:8). The Holy Spirit alighted upon Jesus and Jesus fulfilled the law by obeying the commandments and rejecting sin, established the law.

Jesus came in the likeness of a sinful flesh, meaning the glory Jesus had with God where there was no death, he left that glory and came in the likeness of sinful flesh that perishes. He became the woman and the Holy Spirit alighted upon him through obedience, no razor ever came upon his head, and he was a Nazirite to God from his mother's womb. He was separated for God.

23. Baptism of Jesus

Jesus came from Galilee to John at the Jordan River to be baptized by him. Jesus had never sinned, but He took our sins upon Himself, and to destroy sins, he took baptism. He buried sinful flesh in the water by sacrificing Himself and coming out of the water. The way wheat is sowed, unless it dies, it cannot bear fruit; in the same way, by killing the husband (the devil) of sin gave new birth to the Son and was born again. A natural body is sown, a spiritual body is raised. When He had been baptized, Jesus came up immediately from the water; and behold, the heavens were opened to Him. If you are the son, you are also a joint heir and heaven is open for you (you have access to the Garden of Eden) and a voice came from heaven saying,

"This is My beloved Son, in whom I am well pleased" (Matthew 3:17).

In the same way, if we, women, give birth to a (divine) son, then we can inherit the kingdom with the Son, Jesus. You will also be called the son with Jesus. You will be firstfruits with Jesus. The way the baptism process is, in the same way, Jesus died on the cross and on the third day was risen from the dead. Natural body is sowed, and a spiritual body is raised, and Jesus was raised from the dead through the power of the Holy Spirit. Death could not hold Him and upon being raised from the death, he became the Son of God. Scriptures say, "You are My Son, Today I have begotten You" (Hebrews 5:5).

Thus, Jesus restored the first Adam's status that he had lost. To Adam, the son of God, same as Jesus, the Son of God, God gave Him (His Son) His own kingdom. The son of David will reign forever.

Thank you, God, for bringing us to the kingdom of your beloved Son!

The baptism process and the process of the cross represent death. They represent how the natural body is sowed and after it dies bear fruits.

24. Joseph's Dream

Look, I have dreamed another dream. And this time, the sun, the moon, and the eleven stars bowed down to me said Joseph to his father and brothers. And his father rebuked him saying, "What is this dream that you have dreamed? Shall your mother and I and your brothers indeed come to bow down to the Earth before you?" And his brothers envied him.

Joseph represents Jesus and, within his dream, the sun represents Father, moon the mother, and the eleven stars, the brothers. Joseph's star was lifted high above all the other stars. He was exalted above all. In Joseph's first dream, his sheaf arose upright, and his brothers' sheaves bow down to his sheaf. So,

God exalted Joseph over all his brothers and gave him a name above all names. In the same way, "He (God) has highly exalted Him (Jesus) and given Him the name, which is above every name, that at the name of Jesus every knee should bow, of those in heaven, and of those on Earth, and of those under the Earth" (Philippians 2:9–10).

And Joseph's father Jacob said, "Shall your mother and I come to bow down before you?" And Jacob kept the matter in mind. The sun represents father and it is also a star, but it gives more light as it's near to Earth. Therefore, every tongue should confess that Jesus Christ is Lord of all people to the glory of God the Father.

25. Parable of Resurrection

When Lazarus was sick, his sisters sent message to Jesus that, "He whom you love is sick." When Jesus heard that, He said, "This sickness is not unto death, but for the glory of God, that the Son of God may be glorified through it." Jesus stayed two more days in the place where He was. Jesus said to his disciples, "Lazarus is dead, and I am glad for your sakes that I was not there, that you may believe." When Jesus arrived where Lazarus was, He found that Lazarus had already been in the tomb four days. Jesus said, "I am the resurrection and the life. He who believes in Me, though he may die, he shall live. And whoever lives and believes in Me shall never die."

At Lazarus' grave, Jesus said, "Father, I thank You that You have heard me and with a loud voice said, 'Lazarus, come forth!' And he who had died came out bound hand and foot with graveclothes. Jesus said to them, 'Loose him, and let him go.'"

Thus, if we kill the husband (the devil) of sin (fleshly desires of sin), the way wheat is sown, we who are dead in Christ will be resurrected with Jesus to be firstfruits for the glory of God on the fourth day, which in the fourth millennium means the eighth day. As Jesus said to destroy this temple, and in three days He will raise it up.

As Paul said, at the last trump, the dead in Christ will rise first, meaning those who died to the flesh and its sinful works will rise first and then those who are alive and remaining (whose husband of sin is alive), meaning those who present themselves as living sacrifice which is the church, shall be caught up together with them. We will put on glorified bodies and we shall always be with the Lord.

FOUR

SPIRITUAL LIFE

26. Tree

A tree is shown as a sign for the soul of mankind in the Bible. The way a tree has a life span, mankind also has life span determined for them.

"So He (Jesus) took the blind man by the hand and led him out of the town. And when He had spit on his eyes and put His hands on him, He asked him if he saw anything. And he looked up and said, 'I see men like trees, walking'" (Mark 8:23–24).

Thus, God has planted us on this Earth. Jesus said, "Every plant which my heavenly Father has not planted will be uprooted" (Matthew 15:13). This means works of the flesh, the tares that the Father has not planted, will be uprooted. To those who walk according to the flesh, John the Baptist says, "And even now the ax is laid to the root of the trees. Therefore, every tree which does not bear good fruit is cut down and thrown into the fire" (Luke 3:9).

Nebuchadnezzar's dream that Daniel had interpreted saying, "The tree that you saw, which grew and became strong, whose height reached to the heavens, and which could be seen by all the Earth, is you, O king." Daniel's interpretation determined the tree seen in Nebuchadnezzar's dream represents his life.

Jesus spoke this parable about a certain man who had a fig tree planted in his vineyard. Vineyard represents Israel and the fig tree represents Jesus' soul. God planted Him on this Earth so He can bear fruits.

27. Fig Tree

He also spoke this parable: "A certain man had a fig tree planted in his vineyard, and he came seeking fruit on it and found none. Then he said to the keeper of his vineyard, 'Look, for three years I have come seeking fruit on this fig tree and find none. Cut it down; why does it use up the ground?' But he answered and said to him, 'Sir, let it alone this year also, until I dig around it and fertilize it. And if it bears fruit, well. But if not, after that you can cut it down'" (Luke 13:6–9).

God searches the fig tree for some fruit. The fig tree represents the soul of Jesus. Father God has planted us on this Earth to bear fruits. Three years means for 3,000 years God has searched for a fruit but found none, so Jesus asked for one more year. The fruit which God the Father was searching is the resurrection. This one year is the fourth day (from the birth of Jesus) which is the eighth day (from the beginning), the day of resurrection in the fourth millennium AD. The day of firstfruits is in the fourth millennium AD (after the completion of 7,000 years). The law of circumcision was given for the eighth day, which is the day of resurrection, the day when Jesus raises Lazarus from the dead and says, "Lazarus come forth." In the same way, God will raise us up who are to be the firstfruits with Jesus.

The fruit that God the Father is seeking is resurrection because we are to be firstfruits with Jesus.

28. Fig Tree Cursed

Now the next day, when they had come out from Bethany, He was hungry. And seeing from afar a fig tree having leaves, He went to see if perhaps He would find something on it. When He came to it, He found nothing but leaves, for it was not the season for figs. In response Jesus said to it, 'Let no one eat fruit from you ever again.' And His disciples heard it. (Mark 11:12–14)

Now in the morning, as they passed by, they saw the fig tree dried up from the roots. And Peter, remembering, said to Him, "Rabbi, look! The fig tree which You cursed has withered away." And the scribes and chief priests heard it and sought how they might destroy Him; for they feared Him, because all the people were astonished at His teaching. When evening had come, He went out of the city. (Mark 11:20–21)

The fig tree represents the soul of Jesus, meaning that Jesus had cursed His own soul. It is written, "Cursed is everyone who hangs on a tree" (Galatians 3:13). Jesus took our sins upon Himself and suffered death on the cross and was cursed for us.

Curse means the law. Jesus, through the law, killed his own soul.

Jesus said, "I lay down My life Myself that I may take it again" (John 10:17).

Soul that desires the evil lusts of the flesh. Scripture says that the way wheat is sown and once it dies, the works of flesh dies, only then it bears fruits.

The devil's desire for us is not to bear any fruit for God but, instead, we stay barren. The woman, whose husband is the devil (sin), as long as he lives, she stays barren, as the Scriptures say, "For the desolate has many more children than she who has a husband" (Galatians 4:27).

29. Soul

Per Bible Scriptures, the currency is a symbol of soul.

"When they had come to Capernaum, those who received the temple tax came to Peter and said, 'Does your Teacher not pay the temple tax?' He said, 'Yes.'

And when he had come into the house, Jesus anticipated him, saying, 'What do you think, Simon? From whom do the kings of the Earth take customs or taxes, from their sons or from strangers?' Peter said to Him, 'From strangers.' Jesus said to him, 'Then the sons are free. Nevertheless, lest we offend them, go to the sea, cast in a hook, and take the fish that comes up first. And when you have opened its mouth, you will find a piece of money; take that and give it to them for Me and you'" (Matthew 17:24–27).

Thus, fish and money in the mouth of the fish represent soul.

Luke 19:11–27—The Parable of the Minas

Jesus deposited His soul to the banker so He can receive it back with the interest. *Banker* represents God the Father. Jesus deposited His soul to the banker and redeemed us. As Jesus said, "I have power to lay it down, and I have power to take it again" (John 10:18). As Jesus was crucified on the cross, Barabbas was released which represents the son of man on the cross and the son of the father is released. The name *Barabbas* means "son of the father."

Matthew 20:1–16—The Parable of the Workers in the Vineyard

In the Parable of the Workers in the Vineyard, *friend* represents a prophet. Scriptures say, Abraham was a friend of God. What God was doing, God did not hide from Abraham.

Baruch, who was called a prophet with Jeremiah, who wrote Jeremiah's prophesies in the book of prophecy, when he learned what kind of calamity was going to come upon Israel, (Baruch was an Israelites) God told Baruch, "I will give your life to you as a prize in all places, wherever you go." Thus, the workers in the vineyard are friends of God and He gives each of them a denarius that is their soul.

Thus, all the prophets from Abel to John the Baptist, God has saved their souls and John, the disciple of Jesus, has written this down in the Book of Revelation.

"When He opened the fifth seal, I saw under the altar the souls of those who had been slain for the Word of God and for the testimony which they held. And they cried with a loud voice, saying, 'How long, O Lord, holy and true, until You judge and avenge our blood on those who dwell on the Earth?' Then a white robe was given to each of them; and it was said to them that they should rest a little while longer, until both the number of their fellow servants and their brethren, who would be killed as they were, was completed" (Revelation 6:9–11).

The blood of all the prophets until John the Baptist represents the blood of Abel. Jesus' blood speaks better things than that of Abel. We have forgiveness of sins through the blood of Jesus.

Thus, the souls of the prophets represent currency. Jesus said to render to Caesar the things that are Caesar's, and to God the things that are God's, meaning because we are in the image of God, so we belong to God.

In the Old Testament, Levites were told to redeem the firstborns with the currency (money). This is how the souls of all the people on Earth represent currencies and the life God has given us is God's treasure. As it is written, "Children are an heritage of the LORD: And the fruit of the womb is his reward" (Psalm 127:3 KJV). God wants to gather this heritage in his barn. One world and one currency. Therefore, Jesus gave His life and purchased us. One man dies and not the whole nation perishes.

When a woman finds her lost silver coin, she gathers her friends and rejoices; the same way, when one soul is saved, heaven rejoices. The way when a lost sheep is found, the shepherd rejoices, Jesus came to find which was lost.

30. Prophet

Prophet means a friend of God. Abraham was a prophet; he was a friend of God and God did not hide anything from Abraham. When God came to destroy Sodom and Gomorrah, He made this known to Abraham. Therefore, whatever will happen in the future, God reveals to the prophet. Thus, the prophets from the Old Testament through the Holy Spirit wrote about Jesus' coming.

Prophet also means laborers of the vineyard, which represent the Israelites as they are the vinedressers and the keepers of the vineyard. They are guides for the way to God and they show the direction by prophecies.

Prophet means a friend of the bridegroom, who stands next to him, He prepares the bride for Christ.

Paul says, "Desire spiritual gifts, but especially that you may prophesy so that the one coming in the church may receive the word of knowledge for himself."

There is a difference between the New Testament and Old Testament prophets. According to the Parable of Vineyard, the prophets from Abel to John the Baptist are laborers from early morning. The prophets from the New Testaments are the laborers from the last hour. They all received a denarius and laborers from early morning complained against the landowner, saying that these last men have worked only one hour, and you made them equal to us who have borne the burden and the heat of the day. But he answered one of them and said that, "Friend, I am doing you no wrong." He calls them *friend,* meaning a prophet. The prophets of the Old Testament suffered burden and the heat of the day to receive a denarius, meaning life, but it's easy for the prophets of the New Testament to receive life because of the blood of Jesus and the new covenant. The blood of Jesus covers all of our sins. As David has written, "Blessed is he whose transgression is forgiven, whose sin is covered."

So, Jesus said that the last will be first, and the first last. Because grace and truth came through Jesus Christ.

God saved the souls of the prophets of the Old Testament and John sees them in the revelation under the altar saying, "Judge and avenge our blood on those who dwell on the Earth." Thus, the blood of Jesus speaks better than the blood of Abel. In His blood, there is forgiveness of sins.

Jesus said, "A prophet is not without honor except in his own country and in his own house" (Matthew 13:57).

"I will raise them up a Prophet from among their brethren, like unto thee, and will put my words in his mouth; and he shall speak unto them all that I shall command him. And it shall come to pass, that whosoever will not hearken unto my words which he shall speak in my name, I will require it of him" (Deuteronomy 18:18–19 KJV).

This was a prophecy for Jesus as He Himself is also a prophet. But He was exalted over all His brethren and God has made Him Lord and the Christ. Then, Jesus said to them again, "Most assuredly, I say to you, I am the door of the sheep. All who ever came before Me are thieves and robbers, but the sheep did not hear them" (John 10:7–8).

Whoever came before Me are thieves and robbers, meaning *false prophets* (the devil), who come to steal, kill, and destroy. But the sheep didn't listen to them because they will not listen to the voice of the stranger. The sheep knows the voice of the shepherd and they follow him.

False prophets mean those who lead astray from the way of God. They have climbed up from the other way. The other way is a broad way by which they enter. They enter in the potter's field that was bought by the blood of Jesus to bury strangers. They are dead according to God, so they are buried there.

The way, the rich man was buried, and he was able to see Abraham and Lazarus from there and thirst for the life. He was separated from God for eternity.

And He said to them, "Which of you shall have a friend, and go to him at midnight and say to him, 'Friend, lend me three loaves; for a friend of mine has come to me on his journey, and I have nothing to set before him'; and he will answer from within and say, 'Do not trouble me; the door is now shut, and my children are with me in bed; I cannot rise and give to you'? I say to you, though he will not rise and give to him because he is his friend, yet because of his persistence he will rise and give him as many as he needs" (Luke 11:5–9).

When he asks a friend, a prophet, for bread, he will rise and give him the bread of life as many as he needs, because he is his friend.

31. Temple

Scriptures say that you are the temple of the living God. During Moses' time, when God asked Moses to build a tabernacle, he built the tabernacle as God showed him on the mountain. It is written that the tabernacle was filled with the glory of God. In the same way, we are the temple of God and God lives in us. Therefore, it is also contained in the Scripture, "Behold, I lay in Zion a chief cornerstone, elect, precious, and he who believes on Him will by no means be put to shame" (1 Peter 2:6). Paul says, "Having been built on the foundation of the apostles and prophets, Jesus Christ Himself being the chief cornerstone, in whom the whole building, being fitted together, grows into a holy temple in the Lord, in whom you also are being built together for a dwelling place of God in the Spirit" (Ephesians 2:20–22).

Jesus had PROPHESIZED to them when He said, "Destroy this temple, and in three days I will raise it up" (John 2:19). So, if this temple, the flesh which lusts after sin, is destroyed, in 3,000 years, Jesus Christ will raise it up the way wheat is sowed and bears fruits only after it dies. "It is sown a natural body, it is raised a spiritual body" (1 Corinthians 15:44). The way Jesus said to Lazarus, "come forth" on the fourth day, Jesus Christ and all those who are to be firstfruits with him will come forth (will rise).

"Then Jesus went out and departed from the temple, and His disciples came up to show Him the buildings of the temple. And Jesus said to them, 'Do you not see all these things? Assuredly, I say to you, not one stone shall be left here upon another, that shall not be thrown down'" (Matthew 24:1–2).

"Then Jesus went into the temple of God and drove out all those who bought and sold in the temple and overturned the tables of the money changers and the seats of those who sold doves. And He said to them, 'It is written, "My house shall be called a house of prayer," but you have made it a 'den of thieves'" (Matthew 21:12–13).

Jesus was jealous for the house of God in the same way Elijah was jealous for the God of hosts. After killing 450 prophets of Baal, when Elijah was hiding in the cave and God asked him, "What are you doing here, Elijah?" And he said, "I have been very jealous for the LORD God of hosts" (1 King 19:10 KJV). Thus, Elijah represents Jesus as it's written in the Book of Ecclesiastes that which has been is what will be, that which is done is what will be done.

When Samson was captured by the Philistines and they brought him to the temple of Baal to perform, he prays to God saying, "O Lord God, remember me, I pray! Strengthen me, I pray, just this once, O God, that I may with one blow take vengeance on the Philistines for my two eyes!" And God gives him strength. In the Garden of Gethsemane, an angel of God appeared strengthening Jesus. Samson destroyed the temple of Baal, the den of thieves. The way natural is sowed and spiritual is raised. The visible things will go away, and the spiritual and invisible will last forever because God is a Spirit and so sin and the devil will be destroyed.

They testified against Jesus that, "We heard Him say, 'I will destroy this temple made with hands, and within three days I will build another made without hands'" (Mark 14:58).

Jesus said, "No one can enter a strong man's house and plunder his goods, unless he first binds the strong man. And then he will plunder his house" (Mark 3:27). This house represents us. We are God's house and the strong represents the devil whom we have given authority to our house and have made strong. Jesus is saying to bind that devil with the Word of God.

When Jesus Christ was born on this Earth, He didn't find room in a single house because every house had become a den of thieves, and so he was born in a manger. Jesus said, "Foxes have holes and birds of the air have nests, but the Son of Man has nowhere to lay His head" (Luke 9:58).

There are three sections in the temple. The outer court is for the Gentiles. In this holy place, there are seven lampstands; they represent the church. The holy bread on the table, which is lawful for only the priests to eat, represents the body of Jesus. There also is a golden censer with much incense which represents the prayers of the saints. Those prayers are offered by the priests. As Scriptures say, let my prayer be set before You as incense. The Most Holy, which is the third section in the temple, where the priest goes once a year, is not without blood (of sacrificed animal).

"For no other foundation can anyone lay than that which is laid, which is Jesus Christ. Now if anyone builds on this foundation with gold, silver, precious stones, wood, hay, straw, each one's work will become clear; for the Day will declare it, because it will be revealed by fire; and the fire will test each one's work, of what sort it is. If anyone's work which he has built on it endures, he will receive a reward. If anyone's work is burned, he will suffer loss; but he himself will be saved, yet so as through fire" (1 Corinthians 3:11–15).

God has made a royal priesthood and a holy nation of kings and priests to serve in His temple.

The seven lampstands in the holy place representing the church means priests who present their bodies as living sacrifice, holy and acceptable to God. This is a process. The way we repent from sins and walk in a newness of life is giving up every sin and presenting ourselves acceptable to God.

In the rebellion of Korah, the sons of Ruben rebelled against God, which was why only the sons of Levi serve the Lord; we also will serve the Lord. They represent Jesus. Jesus took our sins upon Himself and rebelled against God to make us a holy priesthood, so that we all can serve the Lord. When God told Moses that any man or beast that comes near the mountain be stoned and killed, that stone represents the law.

But Jesus being from the tribe of Judas climbed the mountain and stood in the midst of the temple. He rebelled against God and qualified us. When Moses lifted the bronze serpent in the wilderness that whosoever believes will not die because of the poison of the serpent but live, in the same way if you present your bodies as a living sacrifice, you will not die but live. That bronze serpent represents God removing sin and cleansing everyone that all can present their bodies as a living sacrifice and serve the Lord. God showed Peter in a vision all kinds of animals in the sheet and said to kill and eat that which God has cleansed and you must not call common. Thus, every nation can serve the Lord.

As it's written, no man or a beast comes near the mountain, but God gave us access to all through Jesus Christ. God commanded Noah to bring clean and unclean animals into the ark. After the Flood, the ark rested on the top of the mountains of Ararat. That is the mountain of God's glory. God came down from the mountain to meet Moses. The Scriptures tell us, "A city that is set on a hill cannot be hidden."

Thus, Jesus cleansed us by his blood so we can present ourselves as living sacrifice, well pleasing to God. The lampstand in the holy place represents the church that repents from their sins and presents themselves to God as living sacrifice, well pleasing to God and God's Holy Spirit stays on that sacrifice as fire.

"The Holy Spirit indicating this, that the way into the Holiest of All was not yet made manifest while the first tabernacle was still standing." (Hebrews 9:8)

When we present our bodies as a living sacrifice, well pleasing to God by killing the husband (the devil) of sin and destroying the first tabernacle (temple), then we will be able to enter the Holiest of All (the Most Holy Place). The way Jesus sacrificed His body, the first temple, is the same as the high priest entering the Holiest of All to God but with His own blood.

The veil of the temple was torn in two from top to bottom. Jesus made a way for us, and we too should enter the Most Holy place with the blood of Jesus. God the Father is in the Most Holy place and that place is for the kings. Jesus made us kings so we can enter the Most Holy and see God.

32. Deep Waters

The Earth was without form, and void; and darkness was on the face of the deep. And the Spirit of God was hovering over the face of the waters. Then God said, "Let there be light and there was light."

Earth without form and void means God was not in it and it did not have life. Because God is the God of order and God said let there be light. In Jesus was life and the life was light of men (John 1:4). Darkness on the face of the deep means water that represents sin. In the deep waters there is darkness. When we get baptized, we bury our sinful flesh in the water and come out of the water and enter in a new life, in the life of light. We enter God's kingdom by being born again.

Scripture says, "When you pass through the waters, I will be with you; And through the rivers, they shall not overflow you" (Isaiah 43:2). If we believe in Jesus, the worldly darkness will not overpower us because God will not let us drown. The Light shines on in the darkness, and the darkness cannot overpower the light.

The way David says, "I walk through the valley of the shadow of death, I will fear no evil for You are with me," so God will be our Shepherd and bring us out from the deep darkness.

In the days of Noah, when God was going to destroy all by the Flood, Noah was building an ark of faith. He was preaching to people the judgment to come but they did not listen to him. In those days, they were marrying and giving in marriage and were one with sin and were experiencing sin. But Noah and seven others in his family were saved through the ark. Besides them, all the people on Earth drowned in the water and died. Noah's ark was on the surface of the waters, meaning it was victorious over sin. The way Jesus never sinned and walked on the water means being victorious over sin. Jesus said, "In this world you will have tribulation, but be of good cheer, I have overcome the world." Jesus marches and leads us to be victorious.

When a baby is in the mother's womb, it's in water, in the darkness, and, when that baby is born, it sees the light. In the same way, when we are in the *deep waters* (sin), we are in darkness and when we come out of the water we see light, meaning we can see God. Jesus said, unless one is born again, he cannot see the kingdom of God. We cannot see God unless we walk in the light.

Job said, "Why was I not hidden like a stillborn child, like infants who never saw light?" (Job 3:16). Job is saying that, the way the stillborn child is in his mother's womb in deep waters, he would have died in darkness. The way people who can never see or know God and perish, Job is saying, it would have been better if he had perished by not being born. In the way the children who have never seen light means never seeing God, never being born again, and not being in existence. Thus, Job curses the day he was born.

Deep waters represent sin. By coming out of sin and being born again, one enters the kingdom of God.

Jesus said that no sign will be given to this generation except the sign of Jonah the Prophet. For, as Jonah was three days and three nights in the belly of the great fish, so will the Son of Man be three days and three nights in the heart of the Earth.

Jonah represents Jesus who was sent to preach. He arose to flee to Tarshish and he was thrown in to the waters. Thus, it pleased the Lord to bruise Him (Jesus). The burden of our sins was laid upon Him and He was thrown into the deep waters, darkness. Thus, Jesus experienced sin in the darkness. The fruit of the tree of the knowledge of good and evil that the woman gave to Adam (Jesus) and He ate. He experienced sin and was separated from God. He was in the belly of the Earth for three days and three nights and prayed and God raised Him up from the dead on the third day. Jonah preached three days in Nineveh to repent and come to God.

Deep waters and darkness represent death. The death that God spoke to Adam and Eve about that in the day you eat of it *you* shall surely die. *Death* means separation from God. Because God is holy and He has no part in the darkness. In the days of Noah, people were marrying and giving in marriage means they were fulfilling lust of the flesh and living in sin. They were careless about themselves and perished. That world was destroyed by the waters the way a stillborn child perishes and never sees the light.

Jonah went down in the deep waters. Scriptures say, "Who will ascend into heaven? (that is, to bring Christ down from above) or who will descend into the abyss? (that is, to bring Christ up from the dead)?" (Romans 10:6). So, Jesus came down from heaven, took our sins, and descended into the abyss. He experienced sin and carried the burden of our sins.

God does not sin, but Jesus descended into the abyss. David said, "If I ascend up into heaven, thou art there: If I make my bed in hell, behold, thou art there" (Psalm 139:8 KJV). God is omnipresent. He is everywhere. Thus, God has experience of both light and the darkness. No place is hidden from Him. There is no place where He cannot be present. Scriptures say, "We are all naked and exposed in His sight." Thus, God is omnipresent.

33. Baptism of the Holy Spirit

"John answered, saying to all, 'I indeed baptize you with water; but One mightier than I is coming, whose sandal strap I am not worthy to loose. He will baptize you with the Holy Spirit and fire.'" (Luke 3:16)

Fire represents purification. If you put gold in fire, it comes out purified. Thus, Peter says, "That the genuineness of your faith is much more precious than gold that perishes" (1 Peter 1:7). The words of the Lord are pure words, like silver tried in a furnace of earth, purified seven times (Psalm 12:6). The Word of God through the fire of the Holy Spirit purifies you and make you holy, the bride wrinkle-free and without blemish for Christ.

Scripture says to present your bodies as living sacrifice, holy, acceptable to God. There is always fire on the sacrifice. We should do good works that are acceptable to God because we are created to do good works in Christ Jesus. Scripture says that anyone who puts his hand to the plow, and looks back, is not fit for the kingdom of God. Thus, whoever is just will continue to be just and whoever is holy be holy still. So, we should continue doing our work faithfully as faithful servants. Do not quench the Holy Spirit but hold fast to holiness.

Ten virgins took their lamps and went out to meet the bridegroom. Now, five of them were wise and five were foolish. Those who did not take their oil means they stopped doing good works. They had to go buy oil for their lamps and the bridegroom came and the door was shut. They came saying, "Lord, Lord, open to us!" But He answered and said, "Assuredly, I say to you, I do not know you." If your lamps went out that means you are in darkness and what communion has the light with darkness? So, Jesus says to them, "I do not know you." Foolish virgins quenched the Spirit when the Scriptures tell us do not quench the Spirit. *Darkness* means sin and if we have communion with sin, we break our relationship with God. If we do not sin, the fire of the Holy Spirit stays on us. If a servant begins to beat his fellow servants in the absence of his master, he is not worthy of the kingdom of God. Our God is a consuming fire and holy.

Abraham said, "How shall I know the future?" So, God asked Abraham to bring Him a three-year-old heifer, a three-year-old female goat, a three-year-old ram, a turtledove, and a young pigeon. Then, he brought all these to Him and cut them in two, down the middle. Now, when the sun was going down, a deep sleep fell upon Abraham; and behold, horror and great darkness fell upon him and when the vultures came down on the carcasses, Abraham drove them away. Because the fire on that sacrifice had gone out and that sacrifice represents Jesus, when Jesus took all of our sins upon Himself on the cross, His fire went out. Scriptures say, "Do not quench the Spirit so God left Jesus." Jesus said, "My God, My God, why have you forsaken Me?" The vultures coming down on the carcasses means, for wherever the carcass is, there the eagles will be gathered together. When Jesus took our sins on the cross, there was darkness for three hours. Death came on Jesus and the sun became black. God, who is light and life, left Jesus.

The way the five virgins' fire went out, we should not quench the fire. Jesus said that whoever blasphemes against the Holy Spirit, will never have forgiveness and the bridegroom will shut the door. The way the door of the ark was closed, and they all drowned and perished.

God purifies us by the fire. When Shadrach, Meshach, and Abednego were thrown into the fiery furnace, the king said to heat the furnace seven times more than it was usually heated. The furnace heated seven times represents perfect purification, where they didn't keep their lives from God. When the servants threw them in the furnace, they saw that they were free and walking in the midst of the fire. The baptism of the fire of the Holy Spirit frees us from all bondages. They see four men walking in the midst of the fire and they said the form of the fourth is like the Son of God. That is Jesus, whose blood covers us, and we are complete through Him. He covers our sin. He makes us strong in our weakness and prepares us to be the bride, who is wrinkle-free and without blemish. He redeems us by His blood.

He purifies us by the fire of the Holy Spirit and makes us holy. Scripture says that when you walk through the fire, you shall not be burned nor shall the flame scorch you. The way Shadrach, Meshach, and Abednego didn't get scorched and burned with the fire. The hair on their head was not singed or their garments affected, and the smell of fire was not on them. God purifies us in a way that doesn't harm us in any way. The way in the chapter of the burning bush, the bush was burning but not being consumed.

34. Thief

"The thief does not come except to steal, and to kill, and to destroy. I have come that they may have life, and that they may have it more abundantly." (John 10:10)

Thus, the devil came to Adam and Eve to steal the place of God. God who was a ruler over us, the devil came to be that ruler.

God had commanded to not eat the fruit of the knowledge of good and evil, meaning not to experience sin. But Adam and Eve disobeyed and experienced sin. God left His place because of sin. The place that was empty the devil took and became ruler over us. Because we broke God's commandment and obeyed the devil's commandments and sinned, slowly by slowly, the devil started to steal everything from within us. He stole love, joy, peace, long-suffering, kindness, goodness, faithfulness, gentleness, self-control from us. The devil brought all kinds of sins within us such as adultery, fornication, uncleanness, lewdness, idolatry, sorcery, hatred, contentions, jealousies, outbursts of wrath, selfish ambitions, dissensions, heresies, envy, murders, drunkenness, revelries, and with these he rules over us.

The devil's intention is to steal the love of God that is within us and the place and authority of God would no longer be there. We would become like the devil, which is complete darkness, and there is no light or life in him.

When God leaves us, we look like the devil. Jesus said to the Pharisees and scribes that you are of your father the devil. When the devil is ruler over us, death reigns in us. We die according to God. He who is a sinner becomes more sinful, the unjust becomes more unjust, and, thus, we keep dying to righteousness.

When we die relative to God, the devil takes us to eternal damnation. When Jesus died on the cross for our sins, God left Him, and He was in the darkness of hell. Jesus didn't commit any sins, so God justified Him and raised Him from the dead and life came back in Him. God became one with Jesus and, by the power of the Holy Spirit, He was raised from the dead. Through the Holy Spirit, who sustained Him in life, He entered life again.

If we go into damnation, there is no hope for us. We will be separated from God forever and will never be one with God.

In the Parable of Abraham and Lazarus, Abraham represents God the Father and Lazarus represents Jesus and all those who will be firstfruits with Him. The rich man, who had pleasure in sin and went to the place of torment, represents those who walked according to the works of the flesh. There was no water of life to drink. He will thirst for that life for eternity but will not receive. On this Earth, he had time to give up his sins and be one with God, but he rejected God and ended up in the place of torment. The rich man was one with the flesh and fulfilled all the lusts of the flesh that resulted in destruction. How much you gain God on this Earth is how much you will receive Him in heaven. In this new creation, there is new heaven and new Earth.

Adam and Eve ate the fruit and put God under feet and the devil on the head. Scriptures say you are the head. We grow in the word means, when we accept God as our ruler, God makes us the head.

35. Tithes

"'Bring all the tithes into the storehouse, that there may be food in My house, and try Me now in this,' says the LORD of hosts, 'If I will not open for you the windows of heaven And pour out for you such blessing That there will not be room enough to receive it.'" (Malachi 3:10)

Give tithes of your income to God and when you give tithes, God increases the fruits of your righteousness. *Temple* means we are the temple of the living God. There may be food in the temple means the food which endures to the everlasting life; labor for that and not for the food that perishes. Thus, there is a roof, a covering of obedience over the temple.

Therefore, give God tithes from your life earnings and the wealth (of sin) of unrighteousness that you have earned, place it on Jesus so that God will bless you with a blessing that there will not be enough room to receive it. He promises you to give the Holy Spirit.

36. Two Witnesses

God wants us to bring all the tithes into the temple so that there may be food in His house and try Him on this and see if God doesn't open for you the windows of heaven and pour out so much blessings for you that there will not be enough room to receive it.

What kind of blessing is that there will not be room enough to receive it? Noah's ark had three parts—the lower, second, and third decks—the way God's tabernacle has three parts—the outer court, the holy place, and the most holy place. Noah's ark had three decks and on the third deck, there was a small window. Noah sends a dove out of the window, and it comes back with a fresh olive leaf in its beak. That dove represents the Holy Spirit. The name *Noah* means "rest." This means that the Holy Spirit finds rest in the olive tree. The two olive trees in the temple represent Moses and Elijah. The Holy Spirit finds rest in these two witnesses.

When Jesus took baptism, the heavens opened, and the Holy Spirit descended in bodily form like a dove upon Him. It is written that Jesus Christ is the faithful witness (Revelation 1:5). He is Moses and Elijah. The Holy Spirit finds rest in Jesus.

When a matter needs to be proved, two witnesses are needed. Thus, Jesus said that I am not alone, the Father who sent Me bears witness of Me. Therefore, to prove Jesus' words, to bear witness and truth, the Father performs miracles. Jesus said if you do not believe Me, believe the works of my father that I do. John the Baptist was the burning and shining lamp who bore witness about Jesus Christ, but Jesus didn't receive his testimony or count on it.

Jesus said, "I am One who bears witness of Myself, and the Father who sent Me bears witness of Me." (John 8:18). Jesus and those who will be firstfruits with Him are the two witnesses who learned Moses' song that is the law and obeyed it.

"And I will give power *to* my two witnesses, and they will prophesy 1,260 days, clothed in sackcloth." (Revelation 11:3)

Sackcloth represents repentance. As Jesus preached to *repent, for the kingdom of heaven is at hand*. Repent from your sins. One thousand two hundred and sixty days, three-and-a-half years, represent 3,500 years. Until the completion of this Earth's life span of 7,000 years and the beginning of the eighth day of circumcision means the new heaven and new Earth, the two witnesses will preach.

"But you shall receive power when the Holy Spirit has come upon you; and you shall be witnesses to Me in Jerusalem, and in all Judea and Samaria, and to the end of the Earth" (Acts 1:8). Disciples witnessed to the end of the Earth and preached the Gospel. "These are the two olive trees and the two lampstands standing before the God of the Earth" (Revelation 11:4). "And if anyone wants to harm them, fire proceeds from their mouth and devours their enemies. And if anyone wants to harm them, he must be killed in this manner" (Revelation 11:5).

On the day of the Pentecost, the Holy Spirit was given to the disciples who were followers of Jesus Christ. "Then there appeared to them divided tongues, as of fire, and one sat upon each of them. And they were all filled with the Holy Spirit and began to speak with other tongues, as the Spirit gave them utterance" (Acts 2:3–4).

Those disciples speak the Word of God through the Holy Spirit. Our God is the God who answers through the fire. Their mouth has the Word of God and fire proceeds from their mouth and devours their enemies mean to destroy sins. They purify people and cause them to die out to sins.

These have power to shut heaven, so that no rain falls in the days of their prophecy. *No rain fall* represents as when Elijah prayed and it did not rain for three-and-a-half years, then he prayed again and it rained. The three-and-a-half years represent 3,500 years when people were under the law. If anyone sinned, God's wrath was revealed in them. But truth and *grace* (rain) came through Jesus Christ. When Ananias keeps part of the proceed from the sale of his land, Peter says that he didn't lie to men but to God and Peter stops the rain of grace on Ananias and Sapphira, meaning they came under the law and the wrath of God was revealed in them and they both died.

Jesus and the followers of Jesus, His disciples, became witnesses through the power of the Holy Spirit, and they are the two olive trees which are in the holy place. They are in the temple and the Holy Spirit finds rest in them.

"They have power over waters to turn them to blood, and to strike the Earth with all plagues, as often as they desire" (Revelation 11:6). The way Moses turned water into blood these two witnesses have power to turn water to blood. Moses represents Jesus.

> On the third day there was a wedding in Cana of Galilee, and the mother of Jesus was there. Now both Jesus and His disciples were invited to the wedding. And when they ran out of wine, the mother of Jesus said to Him, "They have no wine." Jesus said to her, "Woman, what does your concern have to do with Me? My hour has not yet come." His mother said to the servants, "Whatever He says to you, do it." Now there were set there six waterpots of stone, according to the manner of purification of the Jews, containing twenty or thirty gallons apiece. Jesus said to them, "Fill the waterpots with water." And they filled them up to the brim. And He said to them, "Draw some out now, and take it to the master of the feast." And they took it. When the master of the feast had tasted the water that was made wine and did not know where it came from (but the servants who had drawn the water knew), the master of the feast called the bridegroom. And he said to him, "Every man at the beginning sets out the good wine, and when the guests have well drunk, then the inferior. You have kept the good wine until now!" This beginning of signs Jesus did in

Cana of Galilee, and manifested His glory; and His disciples believed in Him. (John 2:1–11)

On the third day, there was a wedding in Cana means during the year 3000s (third millennium AD) there was a wedding. Jesus made wine from water means He made blood from water and gave that blood to the master of the feast. The master of the feast represents God the Father and the master of the feast called the bridegroom and said to him that, "Every man at the beginning sets out the good wine, and when the guests have well drunk, then the inferior. You have kept the good wine until now!" The blood of the animals that was inferior was served until now and you have kept the good blood, meaning the blood of Jesus which is better.

This is the beginning of the signs Jesus did in Cana of Galilee that manifested His glory. By the death of Jesus, He manifested His glory. God glorified the son of man.

Genesis 40:9–22—Butler and Baker's Dreams and Meanings

"And it came to pass after these things, that the butler of the king of Egypt and his baker had offended their lord the king of Egypt. And Pharaoh was wroth against two of his officers, against the chief of the butlers, and against the chief of the bakers. And he put them in ward in the house of the captain of the guard, into the prison, the place where Joseph was bound." (Genesis 40:1–3 KJV)

"And they dreamed a dream both of them, each man his dream in one night, each man according to the interpretation of his dream, the butler and the baker of the king of Egypt, which were bound in the prison." (Genesis 40:5 KJV)

The butler and the baker of the king of Egypt offended the king so he put them in prison. The king of Egypt represents God the Father and they both offended Him. Butler and baker, they both are a service. The *butler* represents the service of offering sacrifice and the *baker* represents serving the belly.

The meaning of the chief butler's dream was three branches of vine that is 3,000 years, it was as though it budded, its blossoms shot forth, and its clusters brought forth ripe grapes. Then he took the grapes and pressed them into Pharaoh's cup. This butler represents Jesus who, by not fulfilling the lust of the flesh, scarified Himself to God. That is Jesus and those who will be firstfruits with Him. *Wine* represents the blood of Jesus, He fills the cup and gives it to the king that is God the Father.

The meaning of the baker's dream is that the baker represents the one who serves his belly and the three baskets are 3,000 years. Three baskets full of bread with the uppermost basket having all kinds of baked goods for Pharaoh but the birds began to eat out of the basket. Those baked goods were for God the Father, meaning our lives belong to God. Scriptures say, "The evil are lazy and serving their own appetites, they fulfill the lust of the flesh."

After three days, God the Father beheaded the baker. Whoever seeks to save his life will lose it, and whoever loses his life will preserve it. But God restored the chief butler (Jesus) to his position, and he placed the cup in Pharaoh's hand.

"When they finish their testimony, the beast that ascends out of the bottomless pit will make war against them, overcome them, and kill them" (Revelation 11:7). The beast makes war with them, conquers them, and kills them. The way Jesus took everyone's sins on Himself and died, He destroyed and removed the sin. The physical body is sowed, and the spiritual is raised. He was dead relative to the flesh but alive relative to the Spirit. When Jesus was on this Earth, He did not commit any sins. He was dead to the works of the flesh and to sin; instead, He was living in the Spirit. Paul said that the world has been crucified to me, and I to the world. Paul means he has no relations with the lust of the flesh and sin; he is dead relative to these.

Dead to works of the flesh and the sin and alive in the Spirit, that's how these two witnesses are. They are dead to sin and flesh but alive in the Spirit as the temple of the living God.

"And their dead bodies will lie in the street of the great city which spiritually is called Sodom and Egypt, where also our Lord was crucified. Then those from the peoples, tribes, tongues, and nations will see their dead bodies three-and-a-half days, and not allow their dead bodies to be put into graves." (Revelation 11:8–9)

They will see their dead bodies three-and-a-half days, meaning for 3,500 years. They are dead to sin, and they witness about God.

Jesus said that if you have love for one another, all will know that you are My disciples. Thus, God is revealed through you. "Now after the three-and-a-half days the breath of life from God entered them, and they stood on their feet, and great fear fell on those who saw them. And they heard a loud voice from heaven saying to them, 'Come up here.' And they ascended to heaven in a cloud, where their enemies saw them" (Revelation 11:11–12).

After three-and-a-half days, meaning 3,500 years, the breath of life from God entered them, meaning the way God raised Jesus from the dead, and they stood on their feet and heard a voice from heaven saying, "Come up here," and they ascended to heaven.

Paul said, "For the trumpet will sound, and the dead will rise first," those who are dead relative to the works of the flesh and sin. The way Jesus died relative to the works of the flesh and sin on the cross, the dead in Christ will rise first. "Blessed and holy is he who has part in the first resurrection. Over such the second death has no power, but they shall be priests of God and of Christ, and shall reign with Him a thousand years" (Revelation 20:6).

Those who are to be firstfruits with Jesus will rise first, over those second death has no power, after that those who are alive who has faith in Jesus Christ and alive relative to His works; they have God's works, the devil cannot kill them, they shall be caught up together with them in the clouds to meet the Lord in the air. And, thus, we shall always be with the Lord.

Elijah asked for fire on the sacrifice and God sent fire from heaven on the sacrifice. This Elijah represents Jesus who said, "I will ask the Father and He will send you the Holy Spirit." By the fire of the Holy Spirit on the sacrifice, Jesus has made us priests to His God the Father. Present your bodies as living sacrifice, holy, acceptable to God. When Jesus transfigured on the mount, Moses and Elijah appeared talking to Jesus. They were talking to Him about Jesus' death, how He will glorify God by His death that is physical death relative to sin which gives glory to God. Those who will be firstfruits with Jesus also give that glory to God.

When Peter, James, and John saw Jesus talking with Moses and Elijah, a bright cloud overshadowed them; and, suddenly, a voice came out of the cloud, saying, "This is My beloved Son, in whom I am well pleased. Hear Him!" Moses had prophesied this, saying that the Lord your God will raise up for you a Prophet like me from your midst, from your brethren. Him you shall hear. These two witnesses are witnesses of the New Testament who are given authority like that of Moses and Elijah.

"And I answered again, and said unto him, 'What be these two olive branches which through the two golden pipes empty the golden oil out of themselves?' And he answered me and said, 'Knowest thou not what these be?' And I said, 'No, my lord.' Then said he, 'These are the two anointed ones, that stand by the Lord of the whole Earth.'" (Zechariah 4:12–14 KJV)

These are the two witnesses who are anointed ones and stand beside the Lord of the whole Earth. God has anointed me as He has anointed them.

Moses parted the Red Sea. God divided waters from waters, symbolizing the separation between physical body and spiritual body—God does not like mixed multitude.

When the prophet Simeon meets Mary, mother of Jesus, he says, "A sword will pierce through your own soul."

"For the Word of God is living and powerful, and sharper than any two-edged sword, piercing even to the division of soul and spirit, and of joints and marrow, and is a discerner of the thoughts and intents of the heart." (Hebrews 4:12)

37. Burden Carrier

> I am not able to bear all these people alone, because it is too heavy for me. (Numbers 11:14 KJV)

> And the LORD said unto Moses, Gather unto me seventy men of the elders of Israel, whom thou knowest to be the elders of the people, and officers over them; and bring them unto the tabernacle of the congregation, that they may stand there with thee. And I will come down and talk with thee there: and I will take of the spirit which is upon thee, and will put it upon them; and they shall bear the burden of the people with thee, that thou bear it not thyself alone. (Numbers 11:16–17 KJV)

Moses represents Jesus who says, "Will you lay the burden of all these people (Israel) on me alone?" So, the burden was also laid on the seventy elders of Israel.

"When Jesus was going to Golgotha carrying the cross, now as they came out, they found a man of Cyrene, Simon by name. Him they compelled to bear His cross" (Matthew 27:32). Thus, he bore the burden of Israel with Jesus.

Now Joshua was old, advanced in years, when he won the Promised Land. He had lot of experience of war. The advanced age and silver-haired head is a crown of glory. Joshua represents Jesus who fought the war and won the Promised Land for us. Scripture says that there remained very much land yet to be possessed and the children of Israel fought the war and possessed the remaining Promised Land. Thus, those who are to be firstfruits with Jesus won the remaining Promised Land.

"But what does the divine response say to him? 'I have reserved for Myself 7,000 men who have not bowed the knee to Baal.'" (Romans 11:4)

Paul says how this is so: It is by the grace of God. For all have sinned and fall short of the glory of God. All submitted to the sin and the devil. Blessed are those whose lawless deeds are forgiven, and whose sins are covered; Blessed is the man to whom the Lord shall not impute sin.

We have forgiveness of sins through the blood of Jesus and our sins are covered. As Jesus, by being obedient, received everything back, those who are to be the firstfruits with Jesus also received everything back and took their place back. All these happened because of grace that 7,000 men didn't bow down to Baal. The 144,000 who learned the song of Moses, and no one else could learn that song, was because of the grace that they are to be firstfruits with Jesus and who has part in the first resurrection with Jesus. This song of Moses is the law that came through Moses. For the law was given through Moses, but grace and truth came through Jesus Christ.

Jesus said, "Shall I not drink the cup which My Father has given Me?" The disciples said they were able to drink the cup also, and Jesus said to them that they will indeed drink the cup that He drinks, and with the baptism He was baptized with they will be baptized. If we suffer with Him, then we are partakers of the suffering and coheirs.

Burden carriers means, as Paul says, "(We are) always carrying about in the body the dying of the Lord Jesus, that the life of Jesus also may be manifested in our body" (2 Corinthians 4:10). This means dead to the works of the flesh, but alive relative to the works of the Holy Spirit.

FIVE

THE SON OF MAN

38. Firstborn

"Then the Lord spoke to Moses, saying, 'Consecrate to Me all the firstborn, whatever opens the womb among the children of Israel, both of man and beast; it is Mine.'" (Exodus 13:1)

"But every firstborn of a donkey you shall redeem with a lamb; and if you will not redeem it, then you shall break its neck. And all the firstborn of man among your sons you shall redeem." (Exodus 13:13)

Every firstborn of a donkey should be redeemed by sacrificing the life of a lamb. All of the firstborn of man should be redeemed, meaning our life has a value. Our life has a value the same as a *talent* (currency) has value; and, to redeem the firstborn, it means redeeming the physical body with a price. Thus, Jesus sacrificed His life and redeemed our physical body. If you do not want to redeem the firstborn of a donkey, you shall break its neck, meaning you should kill him and the yoke on his neck should be broken; when the physical body dies, this means *killing* (destroying) the works of the flesh.

When Jacob took away blessings by deceiving his father Isaac, as God had said the older shall serve the younger, this means the physical body will serve the spiritual body. So, this way, the soul stays under the Spirit. This is how Jesus crushed the devil under His feet by not sinning. For you know that, afterward, when he (Esau) *wanted* to inherit *the blessing*, he was rejected, for he found no place for repentance, though he sought it diligently with tears. Esau sold his birthright for a stew of lentils and, thus, Esau despised his birthright.

Esau represents Jesus, who for the joy that was set before Him endured the cross, despising the shame. Jesus gave His life and gave up His birthright as a firstborn, meaning the physical body is sowed and the spiritual body is raised.

Firstborn means Ishmael who will not be an heir with Isaac. Ishmael represents the physical body which is made of flesh and blood that will not inherit the kingdom of God.

David's firstborn was born through Bathsheba, and God said the child of fornication shall not live, meaning the physical body is sowed and the spiritual body is raised. The second son was Solomon, whose other name *Jedidiah* means "beloved of YHWH." Jesus died on the cross by taking our sins upon Himself. He sacrificed His physical body for us, and the spiritual body was raised. The visible will go away and only the invisible will last.

The firstborn has been compared to a donkey. When Esau said to Isaac, "Bless me also, O my father!" Isaac also blessed him. "Then Isaac his father answered and said to him: 'Behold, your dwelling shall be of the fatness of the Earth, And of the dew of heaven from above. By your sword you shall live, And you shall serve your brother; And it shall come to pass, when you become restless, That you shall break his yoke from your neck'" (Genesis 27:39–40).

Firstborn means the donkey that carries the *yoke* (burdens). Jesus said, "Come to Me, all you who labor and are heavy laden, and I will give you rest. Take My yoke upon you. For My yoke is easy and My burden is light" (Matthew 11:28–29). Scripture says, "His commandments are not burdensome, and His yoke is easy."

When Jesus comes to Jerusalem, he comes riding on a donkey, which represents *burden carrier* (bearer).

Fear not, daughter of Zion; Behold, your King is coming, sitting on a donkey's colt.

When Jesus washed His disciples' feet, He said, "Did you understand what I have done to you? What I am doing you do not understand now, but you will know later on. I did not come to be served but to serve and to be your servant. Whoever follows me will be servant of all."

Paul says that we are always carrying about in the body the dying of the Lord Jesus, that the life of Jesus also may be manifested in our body. The *burden carriers* are those who take care of their spiritual body. The angel of God said about Ishmael that, "He (Ishmael) will be a wild donkey of a man; his hand will be against every man [continually fighting] and every man's hand against him; and he will dwell in defiance of all his brothers" (Genesis 16:12 AMP). Ishmael, wild donkey of a man and his hand shall be against every man and every man's hand against him, means the physical and spiritual are both against each other.

"After him arose Jair, a Gileadite; and he judged Israel twenty-two years. Now he had thirty sons who rode on thirty donkeys; they also had thirty towns, which are called 'Havoth Jair' to this day, which are in the land of Gilead" (Judges 10:3–4). These thirty sons are burden carriers; they represent who carries the yoke.

Gideon had seventy sons who rode on seventy donkeys. Abimelech wanted to be a king over Israel, so he killed seventy sons of Gideon on one stone. Dead according to the flesh but alive according to the Spirit.

After that, when "Abimelech came as far as the tower and fought against it, a certain woman dropped an upper millstone on Abimelech's head and crushed his skull and killed him" (Judges 9:52, 53). Thus, Abimelech died by a hand of a woman.

Abimelech represents Jesus. Jesus wanted to be a king, so he killed his seventy brothers on one stone. This stone is the law, meaning He killed them by the law. Killed according to the flesh but alive according to the Spirit. Jesus also died according to the flesh, the same as His brothers, by stone which is the law. Jesus took our sins upon Himself and took the curse of the law upon Himself. By obeying the law, Jesus fulfilled the law. By not committing even one sin, He destroyed sin. Thus, Jesus died according to the flesh but is alive according to the Spirit. Jesus (Abimelech) was killed by a woman means all of mankind. Woman is a weaker vessel but God's strength was revealed through us weaker vessels that killed Jesus who became sin, killed sin and God gave glory to woman.

Jesus and His seventy brothers who are to be firstfruits with Jesus and will take part in the first resurrection are the ones who are burden carriers. Jesus will be exalted high above all of His brothers. God made Him the King, the Lord, and the Christ and the burden carriers who endure until the end will reign with Jesus.

Samson, who killed 1,000 Philistines with the jawbone of a donkey, is a burden carrier and a firstborn.

When Balaam was going to meet the king and the angel of God stood with a sword on the way and God gave speech to a donkey and donkey spoke. Balaam is a firstborn.

When the firstborn (Jesus) of Pharaoh who sits on his throne, to the firstborn of the female servant and all the firstborns of animals, were killed by God, only then Pharaoh let them go free from slavery. Until the flesh dies to the works of sin, it cannot be free from slavery.

The chariots of Egypt that come after you to make you slaves, you will see them no more because God has destroyed your transgression through Jesus Christ.

39. Knowing God

When the disciples asked what they must do, Jesus said to know God and know the One who He sent that is their work.

To know God means to know that God is a Spirit and to be one with Him in Spirit. Worldly things, evil works, fornication, bitterness, and such should be given up and be one with God to do His works.

As Paul says to not be unequally yoked together with unbelievers this means if you marry, marry within believers and do not be yoked with works of the flesh, but join with the Spirit. By doing this as we obey His commandments, we move towards being one with God. As Jesus said, "My Father and I are One."

When lamps went out for the five foolish virgins, they went to buy oil and the bridegroom closed the door. When foolish virgins said open for us, the bridegroom said, I do not know you, meaning I have never known you because they were not one with Him. I do not know you and I have not known you.

"Strive to enter through the narrow gate, for many, I say to you, will seek to enter and will not be able. When once the Master of the house has risen up and shut the door, and you begin to stand outside and knock at the door, saying, 'Lord, Lord, open for us,' and He will answer and say to you, 'I do not know you, where you are from.'" (Luke 13:24–25)

When people said to Jesus that His mother and His brothers are standing outside, desiring to see Him, Jesus said that those who hear the Word of God and do it are My mother and My brothers. So, Jesus only knows them who keep relationship with God as He has relationship with God. They do according to God's will and commandments and agree with God and obey all His commandments. As Paul says, "What communion has light with darkness?" If your relationship is not with the light that is God, then Jesus does not know you. So, to know God and to keep the relationship with God is our work.

Jesus said that if you abide in Him and He abides in you, you bear much fruit and glorify God. By doing this, we become one in Spirit.

40. Rod of Iron

"You shall break them with a rod of iron; You shall dash them to pieces like a potter's Vessel." (Psalm 2:9)

God's rod is of iron, and He shall dash them to pieces like a potter's vessel, meaning the physical body, which is made of flesh and blood, He will dash it to pieces like a potter's vessel. The physical body is sowed as it will not inherit the kingdom of God and the spiritual body is raised.

Jesus said, "He shall rule them with a rod of iron; They shall be dashed to pieces like the potter's vessels'—as I also have received from My Father." (Revelation 2:27)

Jesus also dashed the vessel of His physical body to pieces like the potter's vessels and received blessings from His Father. Jesus said that all authority has been given to Him in heaven and on Earth.

"Remember your Creator before the silver cord is loosed, Or the golden bowl is broken, Or the pitcher shattered at the fountain, Or the wheel broken at the well." (Ecclesiastes 12:6)

Thus, the pitcher will shatter and the Spirit that God has given you, God will receive back with joy.

When God sends Gideon to fight against the Midianites, he had 32,000 people to fight war. But God said, the people are too many so only 10,000 men stayed and then they were reduced to 300 men. Then, he divided the 300 men into three companies. Then, the three companies blew the trumpets and broke the pitchers—they held the torches in their left hands and the trumpets in their right hands for blowing—and they cried, "The sword of the Lord and of Gideon!" Thus, God gave victory over the Midianites with only 300 men. Three hundred men represent 3,000 years. They broke their pitchers, they dashed their physical bodies into pieces, and they won the battle through the Spirit. Thus, God gave victory with just few men. Gideon represents Jesus.

"And He said to them, 'It is written, My house shall be called a house of prayer,' but you have made it a 'den of thieves.'" (Matthew 21:13)

This house of prayer, the temple, represents our bodies, but we have sinned and are subjected to the devil and worship idols. Every sin is equal to idol worship. Den of thieves that are thieves who rob God. God's work is a work of prayer but, instead, we make the temple a den of thieves to establish our sinful works.

"And Samson called unto the LORD, and said, O Lord GOD, remember me, I pray thee, and strengthen me, I pray thee, only this once, O God, that I may be at once avenged of the Philistines for my two eyes." (Judges 16:28 KJV)

The way Samson prayed to the Lord, and He gave him strength, is the way an angel appeared to Jesus in Gethsemane, giving Him strength. So, God gave Him strength.

Then, with the two pillars which supported the temple, Samson braced himself against them, one on his right and the other on his left. And Samson said, "Let me die with the Philistines!" And he pushed with all his might, and the temple fell. Thus, at his death, he killed the Philistines with himself. Samson represents Jesus who destroyed the temple that was His physical body.

The physical temple, which had the strength of the devil, he destroyed that temple. The way Jesus gave His life on the cross and asked that temple to be destroyed, for in three days He will raise it up. This means, in 3,000 years, Jesus will raise it up on the day of resurrection which is the eighth day in fourth millennium AD. This is also the day of circumcision in which the physical is sowed and the spiritual is raised.

When the disciples came up to show Jesus the buildings of the temple, Jesus said, "I say to you, not one stone shall be left here upon another, that shall not be thrown down." This was a prophecy that Jesus told to His disciples.

> And the whole Earth was of one language, and of one speech. And it came to pass, as they journeyed from the east, that they found a plain in the land of Shinar; and they dwelt there. And they said one to another, Go to, let us make brick, and burn them thoroughly. And they had brick for stone, and slime had they for morter. And they said, Go to, let us build us a city and a tower, whose top may reach unto heaven; and let us make us a name, lest we be scattered abroad upon the face of the whole Earth. And the LORD came down to see the city and the tower, which the children of men builded. And the LORD said, Behold, the people is one, and they have all one language; and this they begin to do: and now nothing will be restrained from them, which they have imagined to do. Go to, let us go down, and there confound their language, that they may not understand one another's speech. So the LORD scattered them abroad from thence upon the face of all the Earth: and they left off to build the city. Therefore is the name of it called Babel; because the LORD did there confound the language of all the Earth: and from thence did the LORD scatter them abroad upon the face of all the Earth. (Genesis 11:1–9 KJV)

When people were building the Tower of Babel, they wanted to reach the heavens, meaning they wanted to reach God's throne and be like God. The tower represents the physical body. At that time, the whole Earth had one language and God saw that the people are one and, now, nothing that they propose to do will be withheld from them. So, God confused their language that they may not understand one another. In this, God is saying that you can become like God, and He will not withhold but reach God not with the flesh but by the Spirit as the works of the flesh are evil.

Thus, God gave us the Holy Spirit and the gift of tongues. In which your physical body cannot take part, but you speak mysteries through the Holy Spirit to God. He who speaks in tongues does not *speak* to men but to God and no one understands him. God says to reach heavens with the Spirit and be like God as God is a Spirit and He never wants you to do sinful works of the flesh but wants you to walk by the Spirit. As many as are led by the Spirit of God, these are the sons of God.

> And the sons of the prophets said unto Elisha, Behold now, the place where we dwell with thee is too strait for us. Let us go, we pray thee, unto Jordan, and take thence every man a beam, and let us make us a place there, where we may dwell. And he answered, Go ye. And one said, Be content, I pray thee, and go with thy servants. And he answered, I will go. So he went with them. And when they came to Jordan, they cut down wood. But as one was felling a beam, the axe head fell into the water: and he cried, and said, Alas, master! for it was borrowed. And the man of God said, Where fell it? And he shewed him the place. And he cut down a stick, and cast it in thither; and the iron did swim. Therefore said he, Take it up to thee. And he put out his hand, and took it. (2 Kings 6:1–7 KJV)

During the time of the prophet Elisha, his disciples went to Jordan to cut down trees to make a place to stay for themselves. While cutting down a tree, the iron ax-head fell into the water and Elisha took a stick and threw it in the water and he made the iron float. The way Jesus walked on the water, He put darkness under His feet. Jesus said that, "In the world you will have tribulation, but be of good cheer, I have overcome the world." The rod of iron belongs to God, and He shall dash and break the potter's vessels. The physical body is sowed and raised in spirit.

The walls of Jericho represent the physical body. When the children of Israel marched around the walls of Jericho for seven days and on the seventh day they shouted, the wall fell. These seven days represent 7,000 years and the walls of the tower of the devil were broken. The physical body is sowed and the spiritual is raised. The eighth day is the day of resurrection. Jesus said, "Destroy this temple and I will raise it up in three days (3000 years)."

41. Son of David

To know the future, when Abraham brought goat and ram, cut them in half and the sun was going down, vultures came down on the carcasses and Abraham drove them away. There appeared a smoking oven and a burning torch that passed between those pieces.

God is saying to Jesus that, "Until a smoking oven and burning torch don't go out, you sit at My right hand. Until the bruised reed will not break, and smoking flax will not quench, you sit at My right hand. Until Death is swallowed up in victory, you sit at My right hand."

"The Lord said to my Lord, 'Sit at My right hand, Till I make your enemies your footstool.'" (Psalm 110:1)

Until the time is fulfilled, the seventh day is fulfilled, until after the seven thousandth year, until the eighth day of resurrection when Jesus and all who will be firstfruits with Jesus are resurrected, and until the new Earth and the new heaven, until the new creation, You (Jesus) sit at My right hand. Until then, God says that you are My Son and today I have begotten you.

God said to David that your son will reign forever. David represents God the Father. Thank God that He received us in His beloved Son's kingdom.

"He will be great and will be called the Son of the Highest; and the Lord God will give Him the throne of His father David. And He will reign over the house of Jacob forever, and of His kingdom there will be no end." (Luke 1:32–33)

"Jesus said to them, 'Assuredly I say to you, that in the regeneration, when the Son of Man sits on the throne of His glory, you who have followed Me will also sit on twelve thrones, judging the twelve tribes of Israel.'" (Matthew 19:28)

Resurrection means new Earth and there will be new heaven where Jesus will sit on the throne of His glory and the son of David will reign forever.

He has made us a holy nation, priests, and kings. Paul says, "You reign that we also might reign with you."

42. Son

No one has seen God at any time. The only begotten Son, who is in the bosom of the Father, He has declared Him. The way Lazarus was in Abraham's bosom. Abraham represents God the Father and Lazarus represents the son. The son who was raised from the dead through the power of the Holy Spirit and sat in His Father's bosom. The son represents Jesus and those who will be firstfruits with Him and they have seen the Father. They are the sons.

God said, "You are my son and today I have begotten you."

Scriptures say, "Whoever sees God, cannot live," meaning he dies to the works of the flesh but lives according to the Spirit.

"For as many as are led by the Spirit of God, these are sons of God." (Romans 8:14)

"Therefore, you are no longer a slave but a son, and if a son, then an heir of God through Christ." (Galatians 4:7)

Paul said, "Not only that, but we also who have the firstfruits of the Spirit, even we ourselves groan within ourselves, eagerly waiting for the adoption, the redemption of our body." (Romans 8:23)

Thus, to be firstfruits, we groan within ourselves in our body. While waiting for the redemption of our bodies, we groan within ourselves means by living in this body, we present our bodies as living sacrifice to God. And, when our husband of sin dies, we become free from the law. And becoming firstfruits, we are redeemed in this body and receive the adoption as the sons.

This is a process. The way there is a lamp in the holy place, presenting your bodies as living and holy sacrifice and destroying the first tabernacle (temple), so that you can enter the Holy of Holies and become the firstfruits with Jesus. All who accepts Jesus Christ go through this process and, by patience glorify God and obtain salvation.

Lot, who was oppressed by the filthy conduct of the wicked for that righteous man tormented his righteous soul from day-to-day by seeing and hearing their lawless deeds, but the Lord knows how to deliver the godly out of temptations. And God delivered Lot and He will also deliver us from this evil world.

Paul says, "I have no commandment for the virgins." *Virgin* means the one whose husband of sin is dead. She is no longer under the law. She is free from the law and, against such, there is no law.

So, the son has no commandment because he is the son. The Levites (the priests) were blameless even when they profane the Sabbath.

Jesus asked Peter, "Whom do the kings of the Earth take customs or taxes, from their sons or from strangers?" Peter said, "Strangers," then Jesus said, "Then the sons are free."

David and the people with him ate the bread that was lawful only for priests to eat.

In Moses' time, daughters asked for their share in the inheritance with their brothers and God gave them their inheritance.

On the Sabbath, disciples began to pluck heads of grain and eat, so the Pharisees said to Jesus that His disciples are breaking the law; but, Jesus said, "I desire mercy and not sacrifice, the Son of Man is also Lord of the Sabbath. The Sabbath was made for man, and not man for the Sabbath."

The sons are free because they have died according to the works of the flesh but are alive to the works of the Spirit.

Son means the man who is in the image of God. "For a man indeed ought not to cover his head, since he is the image and glory of God" (1 Corinthians 11:7). God does not have any ruler over Him, He does not obey anyone's law. So, if a man has long hair, it is a dishonor to him. Thus, man keeps his hair short, representing the likeness of God.

When Abraham asked his servant Eliezer to go and take a wife for Isaac from his country Mesopotamia, Eliezer said, "Perhaps the woman will not be willing to follow me to this land. Must I take your son back to the land from which you came?" Abraham said, "Do not take my son back there from where God brought us out. If the woman is not willing to follow you, then you are released from the oath."

But Jacob, after he deceived his father and took the blessings, went back to Mesopotamia. Where Abraham asked for his son not to go, but Jacob broke that promise and lived in that county for twenty-one years. When Jacob was coming back, he wrestled with the angel of God. The angel of God was stopping him to go back to his country, but the angel did not prevail against him. Jacob asked the angel to bless him, and the angel said, "Your name shall be called Israel, for you have struggled with God and with men and have prevailed." *Israel* means "wrestles with God." The angel touched the socket of Jacob's hip, and the hip was out of joint, and he limped on his hip. The socket of hip (thighbone) represents the promise. Jacob broke the promise, so the angel touched the socket of his hip and the children of Israel do not eat the muscle that shrank. That Israel is the son.

The one who breaks a promise is also a son. Scriptures say, "Kiss the Son, lest He be angry, and you perish in the way, When His wrath is kindled but a little. Blessed are all those who put their trust in Him." (Psalm 2:12)

The son that is Jesus Christ and those who will be firstfruits with Him. Jesus said to His disciples, "If you forgive the sins of any, they are forgiven them; if you retain the sins of any, they are retained" (John 20:23).

When Ananias and Sapphira sell their land and keep part back from the proceeds, Peter says, "Ananias, why has Satan filled your heart to lie to the Holy Spirit and keep back part of the price of the land for yourself?" (Acts 5:3). And Ananias and Sapphira die. Peter is the son. The twelve disciples will sit on the throne with Jesus. Jesus said, "To him who overcomes I will grant to sit with Me on My throne" (Revelation 3:21).

When the soldiers come to take Elijah the Prophet, he said to the captain, "If I am a man of God, then let fire come down from heaven and consume you and your fifty men." And fire came down from heaven and consumed the captain and his fifty. This happened three times.

When youths were mocking Elisha saying, "Go up, you bald-head!" and Elisha was angry and pronounced a curse on them. And two female bears came out of the woods and tore those forty-two youth to pieces. Elisha is the son.

43. Gift of God

The gift of God is Jesus Christ and God has given us His grace for free.

Peter said, "You thought that the gift of God could be purchased with money!" (Acts 8:20). You cannot buy the gift of God. God has given us His gift without any price to us.

The wages of sin is death, but the gift of God is eternal life through Jesus Christ. "For by grace you have been saved through faith, and that not of yourselves; it is the gift of God" (Ephesians 2:8). By faith in Jesus, His blood cleanses us from all sins and makes us holy. Jesus' blood covers all our sins. Scriptures say, "Blessed are those whose lawless deeds are forgiven, and whose sins are covered; Blessed is the man to whom the Lord shall not impute sin" (Romans 4:7–8).

"For if by the one man's offense death reigned through the one, much more those who receive abundance of grace and of the gift of righteousness will reign in life through the One, Jesus Christ. Therefore, as through one man's offense judgment came to all men, resulting in condemnation, even so through one Man's righteous act the free gift came to all men, resulting in justification of life" (Romans 5:17–18).

We have the gift of God, eternal life through faith in Jesus. We have abundant life.

44. Blood of Jesus

"He took bread; and when He had given thanks, He broke it and said, 'Take, eat; this is My body which is broken for you; do this in remembrance of Me.'" (1 Corinthians 11:24)

This means Jesus sacrificed His physical body for us. He loved us so much that He gave up His immortal body and became mortal when He came in the likeness of sinful flesh and sacrificed Himself so that we can be free from the slavery of sin.

"In the same manner He also took the cup after supper, saying, 'This cup is the new covenant in My blood. This do, as often as you drink it, in remembrance of Me.'" (1 Corinthians 11:25)

"Therefore, brethren, having boldness to enter the Holiest by the blood of Jesus." (Hebrews 10:19)

Jesus made a new covenant with us, whatever was becoming obsolete and growing old is ready to vanish away, so He made a new covenant (made all things new). He gave His life and brought death to sin. God punished sin in His body and destroyed sin.

Thus, when we eat the bread that represents Jesus' body and drink the cup that represents His blood, and take communion, it brings death to sin in our bodies.

"Jesus said to them, 'Most assuredly, I say to you, unless you eat the flesh of the Son of Man and drink His blood, you have no life in you'" (John 6:53). Thus, we should partake of the cup and walk in the light. Without this, Jesus' life is not revealed through us.

"Therefore, brethren, having boldness to enter the Holiest by the blood of Jesus, by a new and living way which He consecrated for us, through the veil, that is, His flesh" (Hebrews 10:19–20). We can see God. Jesus said, "If you have seen me, you have seen the Father." Blood of Jesus cleanses us from all sins.

"And they sang a new song, saying: 'You are worthy to take the scroll, and to open its seals; For You were slain, And have redeemed us to God by Your blood Out of every tribe and tongue and people and nation.'" (Revelation 5:9)

Jesus, by His own blood, bought all the people of the Earth for God. Whoever believes in Jesus, they are purchased of God and whoever doesn't believe in Jesus are the Gentiles. They were also bought with a price.

It's written that the price Judas received to betray Jesus when he brought it back to the chief priests is that they took the silver pieces and said that it is not lawful to put them into the treasury because they are the price of blood. Then, they consulted together and bought with them the potter's field to bury strangers in. This means the Gentiles who are dead to the works of God, dead to God, the field was bought for them so that they can be buried there.

"So Sarah died in Kirjath Arba (that is, Hebron) in the land of Canaan, and Abraham came to mourn for Sarah and to weep for her." (Genesis 23:2)

Abraham (God the Father) said to the sons of Heth, "If it is your wish that I bury my dead out of my sight, hear me, and meet with Ephron the son of Zohar for me, that he may give me the cave of Machpelah which he has, which is at the end of his field. Let him give it to me at the full price, as property for a burial place among you."

Thus, Abraham bought the land for 400 shekels of silver from Ephron to bury his dead. Therefore, those who are dead according to the works of God, land has been bought to bury them. The way the rich man died, and he was buried.

There is a temple and as the outer court is given to the Gentiles, the most holy place and the holy place are for the people of God where God is; in the same way, Lazarus and the rich man were after their death. Lazarus, who is the son of God, in Abraham's bosom means in God's bosom that is Jesus and those who will be firstfruits with Him, who obtained the first resurrection and are in God's bosom. And the rich man is in the outer court which God bought with a price to bury strangers in. There is great gulf fixed between Lazarus and the rich man. No one can pass through that great gulf to go there or from there to here. Thus, the Gentiles will see God and see Lazarus and they will be tormented. Because they wasted their lives that God had given them on this Earth for useless things, but Lazarus spent his life to obtain God. And Lazarus was in a place of comfort in God's bosom, which was a reward for the pain he suffered to be born again, that reward was God. As God told Abraham, "I am your shield and your exceedingly great reward." That God is our inheritance. The way God told the Levites, "I am your inheritance."

Scriptures say, "Every knee shall bow, and every tongue shall confess to God that Jesus Christ is Lord, to the glory of God the Father." So, all Gentiles will confess the same. Every eye will see Him, and all elders will cast their crowns and say, "You are worthy, O Lord, to receive glory and honor and power; For You created all things, and by Your will they exist and were created" (Revelation 4:11).

45. Jesus' Coming Leading to Life

> Now learn this parable from the fig tree: When its branch has already become tender and puts forth leaves, you know that summer is near. So, you also, when you see all these things, know that it is near—at the doors! Assuredly, I say to you, this generation will by no means pass away till all these things take place. Heaven and Earth will pass away, but My words will by no means pass away. (Matthew 245:32–35)

Jesus said, assuredly, I say to you, this generation will by no means pass away till all these things take place. All things said by Jesus will by no means pass way without taking place in each person's life. Jesus' coming takes place in each person's life individually. And Jesus gives rewards to each according to his or her works. If you have done good works through faith in Jesus, you will receive your reward on this Earth. The way Joseph was faithful to God and when the time came God made him equal to Pharaoh and exalted and honored him. Joseph represents Jesus who was in prison without any fault, as also Jesus took our sins and died, but on the third day He was exalted and seated on the right hand of God and received His glory and honor. He was made to be equal to God.

We know that "Jesus' Coming" happened in eleven disciples' lives, and Jesus gave the disciples rewards according to the works of their hands. People were healed by the shadow of Peter and God was testifying and showing signs and miracles to prove the truth of the Gospel that what the disciples were teaching was the truth.

Luke 19:11–27—Parable of Minas Explanation

Jesus said in a parable, "A certain nobleman went into a far country to receive for himself a kingdom and to return. So, he called ten of his servants, delivered to them ten minas, and said to them, 'Do business till I come'" (Luke 19:12–13). One mina to one servant represents each soul. But his citizens hated him, and sent a delegation after him, saying that we will not have this man to reign over us. When he returned, having the kingdom, means when Jesus returned, He asked his servants how much every man had gained by trading. The first said that one mina has earned ten minas, the second servant gained five minas, and the third servant said, "Master, here is your mina, which I have kept put away in a handkerchief." So, the life that God has given us is to do good works in Christ Jesus and that's why we are created. Our work is to know God and to know the One God sent. But this servant didn't do any of this work.

If you walk according to the flesh, you will receive reward according to those works. God's wrath that has been reserved for those who do not obey, that they will receive in this lifetime and also in the new age to come.

When Jesus comes, we will rise either leading to life or leading to death.

"But of that day and hour no one knows, not even the angels of heaven, but My Father only" (Matthew 24:36). This means when God the Father sends Jesus, He establishes His Kingdom as king within us. And those who walk according to the flesh, He gives them reward according to their works.

"For the Son of Man will come in the glory of His Father with His angels, and then He will reward each according to his works." (Matthew 16:27)

Jesus said, "The kingdom of God does not come with observation; nor will they say, 'See here!' or 'See there!' For indeed, the kingdom of God is within you" (Luke 17:20–21). God's kingdom doesn't come with observation, but it comes within you.

"Then Peter began to say to Him, 'See, we have left all and followed You.' So Jesus answered and said, 'Assuredly, I say to you, there is no one who has left house or brothers or sisters or father or mother or wife or children or lands, for My sake and the Gospel's, who shall not receive a hundredfold now in this time—houses and brothers and sisters and mothers and children and lands, with persecutions—and in the age to come, eternal life.'" (Mark 10:28–30)

When Jesus appeared in the disciples' lives, it was not with observation but when they were faithful in their lives as the servant who being faithful earned ten minas from one and he was given authority over ten cities, the disciples were also given authority over many, Jesus gave them reward for the works of their hands. People were healed by Peter's shadow. People of the Early Church were selling all their possessions and laying the proceed at Peter's feet. Paul said that you have reigned as kings, and we also might reign with you. "And He (God) raised us up together and made us sit together in the heavenly places in Christ Jesus" (Ephesians 2:6). God gave Adam and Eve authority over the Earth but to Peter God gave the keys of the kingdom of heaven. Jesus said, "All authority has been given to Me in heaven and on Earth."

"To him who overcomes I will grant to sit with Me on My throne. Thus, we rule with Him in this life and in life to come."

"And now, little children, abide in Him, that when He appears, we may have confidence and not be ashamed before Him at His coming." (1 John 2:28)

This is a parable about Jesus' coming. A certain nobleman called ten of his servants, delivered to them ten minas, and said to them, "Do business till I come." *Minas* represent our lives. This is how God the Father has given us life that we do the works of God and give glory to God. But his citizens hated him, and sent a delegation after him, saying, "We will not have this man to reign over us." They did not want to do God's work but enjoyed in the works of the flesh.

And so it was that when he returned, having received the kingdom, he called the servants and asked them to give accounts, meaning we are asked for an account of our lives. When Jesus comes in our lives, He will ask each of us to give an account of ourselves. If we say, my mina has earned ten minas, He will commend us and, for our faithfulness, He will give us authority over much more. But to those who did not want Him to rule over them, He will kill them, meaning they will receive reward leading to death in this life, God's wrath will be revealed in their lives. And, in the life to come, there will be *second death*, which is separation from God forever.

Jesus' coming won't be sudden to those who are the sons of the light, but the day will come suddenly as a thief to the sons of the darkness. We will be able to see the kingdom of God coming within us, but the people in darkness won't know it.

> And the Lord said, "Who then is that faithful and wise steward, whom his master will make ruler over his household, to give them their portion of food in due season? Blessed is that servant whom his master will find so doing when he comes. Truly, I say to you that he will make him ruler over all that he has. But if that servant says in his heart, 'My master is delaying his coming,' and begins to beat the male and female servants, and to eat and drink and be drunk, the master of that servant will come on a day when he is not looking for him, and at an hour when he is not aware, and will cut him in two and appoint him his portion with the unbelievers. And that servant who knew his master's will, and did not prepare himself or do according to his will, shall be beaten with many stripes. But he who did not know, yet committed things deserving of stripes, shall be beaten with few. For everyone to whom much is given, from him much will be required; and to whom much has been committed, of him they will ask the more."(Luke 12:42–48)

The Lord said, "Who then is that faithful and wise steward, whom his master will make ruler over his household, to give them their portion of food in due season? Blessed is that servant whom his master will find so doing when he comes." If we are faithful to Him and patiently bear fruits, we will surely receive the reward. But, if that servant says in his heart, "My master is delaying his coming" and begins to beat the male and female servants, and to eat and drink and be drunk, the master of that servant will come on a day when he is not looking for him, and at an hour when he is not aware, and will cut him in two and appoint him his portion with the unbelievers. Thus, he will be cut off from the people of God and his portion will be separation from God for eternity. Whatever is committed to each person, it will be required from him.

Matthew 25:1–13—Explanation of the Parable of the Wise and Foolish Virgins

Then the kingdom of heaven shall be likened to ten virgins who took their lamps and went out to meet the bridegroom. Now five of them were wise, and five were foolish. The foolish didn't take oil with them; *oil* represents righteous works for God. So, the oil ran out while the bridegroom was delayed, Jesus' coming in their lives was delayed and, while they went out to buy oil, the bridegroom came. But the foolish virgins were not in their place, the way the angels who did not keep their proper domain. But the wise virgins went with the bridegroom leading to life and the door was shut.

During the times of Noah, people didn't listen to righteous Noah's warnings and few with Noah were saved through the ark and others were destroyed by the Flood. When the foolish virgins came back with the oil and said, "Lord, Lord, open to us," but he answered and said that "Assuredly, I say to you, I do not know you." If you do not have works of God, He does not know you. And, after Jesus' coming in your life, if you prepare yourself and bring lots of oil, but the time is over and there is no hope for you. Watch, therefore, for you know neither the day nor the hour in which the Son of Man is coming.

When Jesus appears, then two men will be in the field: one will be taken and the other left. Two women will be grinding at the mill: one will be taken and the other left (Matthew 24:40–41). This means some will enter the kingdom of God and some will be left out and be separated from God for eternity.

Even so will it be on the day when the Son of Man is revealed. "In that day, he who is on the housetop, and his goods are in the house, let him not come down to take them away. And likewise, the one who is in the field, let him not turn back.

Remember Lot's wife. Whoever seeks to save his life will lose it, and whoever loses his life will preserve it" (Luke 17:30–33).

The day Son of Man is revealed, it will happen that whoever is on the housetop and his goods are in the house, should not come down to take them away. *Housetop* represents a spiritual status, a status of higher level. The way, one evening, Davis was on the roof of the house and David represents God the Father. He should not come down from his place. He, who is in the field, let him not turn back, meaning the laborers in the field are the servants of God to do His work. The prophets who should continue to do God's work and not turn back. Remember Lot's wife. No one, having put his hand to the *plow*, and looking back, is fit for the kingdom of God.

"For the Lord Himself will descend from heaven with a shout, with the voice of an archangel, and with the trumpet of God. And the dead in Christ will rise first. Then we who are alive and remain shall be caught up together with them in the clouds to meet the Lord in the air. And thus we shall always be with the Lord." (1 Thessalonians 4:16–17)

The dead in Christ will rise first, meaning those who have killed the husband of sin (the devil) and those who are dead to the works of the devil; those who are slain for Christ will rise first. The way Jesus was raised from the dead; the way Elijah, who represents Jesus, was taken up to heaven in a whirlwind. Jesus, after He rose from the dead through the power of the Holy Spirit, was seen by more than 500 brethren and then was lifted up to the Father in heaven. Thus, we who are slain will be raised with Jesus Christ when Jesus appears in our lives.

And those who are alive who have not killed the husband of sin but are alive to God, those who present their bodies as acceptable and living sacrifice to God in the holy place, for them, Jesus says, "Those who are alive for me, they will never die, death will not prevail against them." The way Enoch walked with God and God took him alive, in the same way those that are alive will be.

Thus, the disciples and the first church experienced the coming of Jesus and the first resurrection of their bodies. When the Pharisees put the disciples in prison and God freed them and said to the disciples, "Go, stand in the temple, and speak to the people all the words of this life," the officer couldn't find them in the prison and said, "We found the prison shut securely, and the guards standing outside before the doors, but when we opened them, we found no one inside!" Thus, the disciples experienced the glorified body in the same way Jesus did when He appeared to the disciples in the room with closed doors and talked with them. The disciples came out from the prison that was securely shut.

Thus, Paul writes that those who have experienced the new age to come, miracles, healings, promises, resurrection, that age in new creation, new heaven, and new Earth, after experiencing all these, if we sin, there no longer remains a sacrifice for us. *Healing* represents there is no sickness in heaven, in the new creation that will be after 7,000 years of this Earth is completed and when the year 8000 starts (the fourth millennium AD). The new heaven and new Earth, Jesus said, "See I make all things new." The eighth day of circumcision is the day of resurrection.

Joseph represents Jesus. In Joseph's dream, sheaves of all his eleven brothers bowed down to his sheaf and, in his second dream, the sun, moon, and all the stars bowed down to him.

Brothers' sheaves in the field that bowed down represent those who have not killed the husband of sin and are alive. They are connected to the Earth, connected to the flesh. They represent those who have not destroyed the works of the flesh completely; they will live on the Earth which will be a new Earth.

But the stars of heaven represent those who have killed the husband of sin. They have destroyed the works of sin and are dead to flesh. As Paul says, "The world has been crucified to me and I to the world." They are of heaven; they are the 144,000. They are the bride of Christ who is without wrinkle or blemish. They will receive the sign of circumcision, which is the sign of perfection, and they will be firstfruits with Christ. The eighth day is the day of the resurrection and the stars of heaven will bow down to Jesus of heaven.

Scriptures say, "At the name of Jesus every knee should bow, of those in heaven, and of those on Earth, and of those under the Earth" (Philippians 2:10).

Those who are from under the Earth, who are in darkness, have never seen God and some who have seen have chosen darkness as the five foolish virgins did. Those people will be separated from God forever. They will also bow down to Jesus and confess that Jesus is the Lord. Thus, those in heaven, those on Earth, and those under the Earth are different people.

Those who are from under the Earth, they have chosen darkness instead of the light. God's wrath will come on those when Jesus comes in their lives as a thief. Then, God will give them reward for the works of their hands leading to death and God's wrath will be revealed in them. When an unclean spirit was cast out from a man, that unclean spirit comes back and sees the place swept and put in order, he goes and brings seven other spirits more wicked than himself, and the last state of that man is worse than the first. This will be the state of those who have rejected God.

We experience the age to come in our lives on this Earth. We experience Jesus' coming in our lives and the resurrected life. When the eighth day starts in the fourth millennium AD, the last day will come, the Lord Himself will descend from heaven with a shout, with the voice of an archangel, and with the trumpet of God. And the dead in Christ will rise first. Those who have died to the works of the flesh, they will rise first. Then, we who are alive and remain shall be caught up together with them in the clouds to meet the Lord in the air. Those who are alive to works of God but have not killed the husband of sin but alive to God. They will be caught up together with them and, thus, we shall always be with the Lord. Thus, we will be glorified in the age to come.

Then, new heaven and new Earth. All things visible will go away and only the invisible will last, meaning the spiritual lives will last.

"He will be great, and will be called the Son of the Highest; and the Lord God will give Him the throne of His father David" (Luke 1:32). Thus, Jesus and those who will be firstfruits with Him will reign in the new age.

46. Shefali's Coming of Christ

Shefali is my biological sister. In those days, Shefali was talking a lot to me about Jesus' coming. She was also talking a lot about prophesies. During that time, I had a dream about her. In that dream, I went to her house and her house was a big, white-colored, two-story house. All the furniture and sofas in her house were white. I went to the second floor of her house, and it had a big balcony and I stood there and was looking far away in the sky. I saw angels coming toward the house. They were far away in the sky, so they look very small. They were many angels. They were coming as though Jesus' coming was happening. They were coming toward Shefali's house, and I immediately turned my face away and my dream ended. Thus, God showed me Jesus' coming that was going to happen in her life.

47. Jesus' Coming in My (Sejal's) Life

My biological sister, Shefali, was talking to me about Jesus' coming a lot, that Jesus Christ is coming soon. One day, she called me over the phone, and I was listening to her. I was sitting in my bedroom and, all of a sudden, I had a vision and I looked into the sky and saw Jesus Christ on a white horse, He was wearing a white robe and long blue blazer on top of the white robe. He was wearing leather sandals on His feet, and He had a heavy gold crown on His head. There were thick white clouds surrounding Him. And Jesus Christ lifted His hand and said to me, "I am coming." And my vision ended. And I started thinking that Jesus said to me "I am coming," but He didn't say "soon."

After that vision, a few days later, I was working at my job and praying in tongues quietly while working. During that time, I felt something heavy on my head and I started thinking what it is. Immediately, I had a vision and I saw a crown on my head that was the same crown I saw Jesus wearing in my vision and I was able to feel that. Then, I realized that Jesus has come in my life as the King. Thus, we are to rule with Jesus.

Scriptures say that when the Son of Man comes in His glory, He will give each according to the works of their hands. Thus, He gave me this book to write and the ministry to raise the dead.

"It is the glory of God to conceal a matter, But the glory of kings is to search out a matter." (Proverbs 25:2)

All the revelations in this book that God the Father has given me to write down He has explained them to me. He has spoken to me and let me write this book. I want to give all the glory to God our Father.

48. Jesus' Coming Leading to Death

God gave us this life. God has planted us on this Earth so that we do works of God and glorify Him. Scripture says, "Esau sold his firstborn birthright that is his physical body to Jacob for stew of lentils, he sold the life God had given him." Thus, he despised his firstborn birthright.

Paul says, "Esau, who for one morsel of food sold his birthright. For you know that afterward, when he wanted to inherit the blessing, he was rejected, for he found no place for repentance, though he sought it diligently with tears" (Hebrews 12:16–17).

In the same way, we accepted Jesus and saw the light and, then, if we turn back, there won't be any place for repentance. As Jesus said, "No one having put his hand to the plow, and looking back, is fit for the kingdom of God." The way Lot's wife looked back and became a pillar of salt, when Jesus comes, whoever is in the field should stay there because he is God's laborer and is working for God; whoever is in the way, flee to the mountains, meaning to go to glory; whoever is on the housetop should not come down. The work you are doing in Christ, keep on doing and do not turn back.

Paul says, "For it is impossible for those who were once enlightened, and have tasted the heavenly gift, and have become partakers of the Holy Spirit, and have tasted the good Word of God and the powers of the age to come, if they fall away, to renew them again to repentance, since they crucify again for themselves the Son of God and put Him to an open shame" (Hebrews 6:4–6).

As the ten virgins went out to meet the bridegroom and, when Jesus arrived, the foolish ones were not in their place, they went back because they ran out of oil. They had stopped doing the righteous works so that their lamps went out, the fire of the Holy Spirit went out. Then, they came back with the oil, but the door was closed. They asked to open the door, but the bridegroom said, "I do not know you." Likewise, "If that evil servant says in his heart, 'My master is delaying his coming,' and begins to beat his fellow servants, and to eat and drink with the drunkards, the master of that servant will come on a day when he is not looking for him and at an hour that he is not aware of and will cut him in two and appoint him his portion with the hypocrites. There shall be weeping and gnashing of teeth" (Matthew 24:48–51).

Jesus also says, "Woe to you, Chorazin! Woe to you, Bethsaida! For if the mighty works which were done in you had been done in Tyre and Sidon, they would have repented long ago, sitting in sackcloth and ashes. But it will be more tolerable for Tyre and Sidon at the judgment than for you" (Luke 10:13–14).

Jesus said, "When an unclean spirit goes out of a man, he goes through dry places, seeking rest, and finds none. Then he says, 'I will return to my house from which I came.' And when he comes, he finds it empty, swept, and put in order. Then he goes and takes with him seven other spirits more wicked than himself, and they enter and dwell there; and the last state of that man is worse than the first. So shall it also be with this wicked generation" (Matthew 12:43–45).

When Jesus comes back in each one's life, it is either leading to life or leading to death. To those leading to death will be separated from God forever. As the door was closed for the foolish virgins and was not opened, as the door of Noah's ark was shut by God, they will perish and will be separated from God forever. After that, there won't be any place for repentance and the door will not be opened.

Dead means those who are dead to the works of God. They will be judged by their works. "The sea gave up the dead who were in it, and Death and Hades delivered up the dead who were in them. And they were judged, each one according to his works. Then Death and Hades were cast into the lake of fire. This is the second death" (Revelation 20:13–14).

"Women received their dead raised to life again" (Hebrews 11:35) means those who lose their lives will save it. Thus, they who were dead according to the flesh, they received their life again. The way God raised Jesus Christ from the dead, God will change our mortal bodies to the glorified bodies. Jesus said to the Sadducees that in the resurrection they neither marry nor are given in marriage, but are like angels of God in heaven.

Those who are resurrected leading to death are those who are dead to the works of God. They will rise and God will give them reward for their evil works according to the flesh. God's wrath is for those whose pitcher is full of sins, and God's wrath will not delay. Because God has suffered patiently and waited to pour out His bowls of wrath. Paul says, "But in accordance with your hardness and your impenitent heart you are treasuring up for yourself wrath in the day of wrath and revelation of the righteous judgment of God" (Romans 2:5).

This wrath of God, when the Son of Man, Jesus, comes with the glory of His Father, He will give full reward to each one according to their works. Thus, His coming happens in each individual's life and everyone receives the reward according to the works of their hands in this life and also in the life to come.

When John the Baptist saw many of the Pharisees and Sadducees coming to his baptism, he said to them, "Brood of vipers! who warned you to flee from the wrath to come?"

God's wrath reveals in those who are perishing. They receive reward for their evil works.

Scripture says, "For God so loved the world that He gave His only begotten Son, that whoever believes in Him should not perish but have everlasting life. For God did not send His Son into the world to condemn the world, but that the world through Him might be saved" (John 3:16–17).

After seeing the light, if we reject the light, then we are condemned already. Today, if we accept Jesus, we will be saved from the wrath of God. Today is the day of acceptance; today is the day of salvation. We should not neglect God's grace and truth to be saved.

49. Lamentations of God

"A voice was heard in Ramah, lamentation, weeping, and great mourning, Rachel weeping for her children, refusing to be comforted, because they are no more." (Matthew 2:18)

God is lamenting for His children because they are separated from Him forever. Jesus said, "Those whom You gave Me I have kept; and none of them is lost except the son of perdition" (John 17:12).

Judas Iscariot, who sold Jesus, represents the son of perdition, those who walked according to their flesh and sold their own bodies to the devil. The way Esau sold his firstborn birthright for a stew of lentils, he despised his physical body and gave up his physical body in vain. In the same way, those who choose darkness instead of the light and live in their sins, they also despise their physical body. In the days of Noah, people were marrying and giving in marriage and being one with sinful flesh. Those who cheat cheat themselves when they lie in wait to shed blood; they lurk secretly for their own lives.

Those who satisfy their belly, meaning the lust of the flesh, they will perish. As it's written, Judas Iscariot purchased a field with the wages of iniquity; and, falling headlong, he burst open in the middle and all his entrails gushed out. He died because of fulfilling the lust of his belly. He burst open in the middle means his belly burst open and his entrails gushed out and he perished.

Judas Iscariot hanged himself and died means he destroyed himself on his own. In the same way, those who sin reap destructions for themselves.

Those who lust after the flesh, they destroy God's Seed that is Jesus Christ from within them and bring death to the Seed and the life that was in them; they reject that life. Thus, they sell Jesus to the devil and betray Him.

When Joab, a commander over the army of Israel, stabs Abner in the stomach and he dies; the way Judas Iscariot died, Abner dies in the same way. "And afterward when David heard it, he said, I and my kingdom are guiltless before the LORD for ever from the blood of Abner the son of Ner" (2 Samuel 3:28 KJV).

David represents God the Father who declares Himself guiltless forever regarding the blood of the son of perdition.

Thus, David (God) lamented for Abner. "And they buried Abner in Hebron: and the king lifted up his voice, and wept at the grave of Abner; and all the people wept" (2 Samuel 3:32 KJV).

The king (God the Father) lamented for the son of perdition and said, "Should Abner die as a fool dies? Your hands were not bound, nor your feet put into fetters; As a man falls before wicked men, so you fell" (2 Samuel 3:34–37).

We, as fools, shouldn't let ourselves perish but live to God and inherit eternal heritage. Those who perish, God is not guilty for them. We ourselves by lust of the flesh conceive sin and give birth to the son of perdition and bring destruction.

> And they sent the coat of many colours, and they brought it to their father; and said, This have we found: know now whether it be thy son's coat or no. And he knew it, and said, It is my son's coat; an evil beast hath devoured him; Joseph is without doubt rent in pieces. And Jacob rent his clothes, and put sackcloth upon his loins, and mourned for his son many days. And all his sons and all his daughters rose up to comfort him; but he refused to be comforted; and he said, For I will go down into the grave unto my son mourning. Thus his father wept for him. (Genesis 37:32–35 KJV)

Thus, God the Father wept for those who are perishing.

50. Life of Mankind

"All flesh is as grass, and all the glory of man as the flower of the grass. The grass withers, and its flower falls away, but the word of the Lord endures forever. Now this is the word which by the Gospel was preached to you." (1 Peter 1:24–25)

The life of mankind is temporary, today is and vanishes tomorrow. The physical body is for a short time. Scripture says, "We are voyagers on this Earth for a short time."

But the Word of God lasts for eternity. The life of mankind is like a vapor that appears in the morning for a short time and then vanishes away in the afternoon.

Whatever is visible is perishable and the invisible is for eternity. So, we should not love this world and the things of this world. The love of this world and things of the world is enmity with God. "Set your mind on things above, not on things of this Earth" (Colossians 3:2).

Jesus said, "Do not labor for the food which perishes, but for the food which endures to everlasting life." There is no profit from the flesh and the blood. The glory of man's life is perishable. There is no profit from the lusts of the flesh.

"The ground of a certain rich man yielded plentifully. And he thought within himself, I will pull down my barns and build greater, and there I will store all my crops and my goods. But God said to him, 'Fool! This night your soul will be required of you; then whose will those things be which you have provided?'" (Luke 12). Thus, if we walk by the flesh, we will perish; because works of the flesh are only until this physical body lasts, after that, they perish as they are only temporary. But, if we walk by the Spirit, God will give us everlasting life that will never end.

Jesus said to Nicodemus, "Most assuredly, I say to you, unless one is born again, he cannot see the kingdom of God." The one born according to the flesh is flesh and the one born according to the Spirit is spirit. From Adam to John the Baptist, all of the people from the Old Testament are born according to the flesh. They are followers of the law. By faith in Jesus, the people that follow Jesus are people from the New Testament. Jesus said, "You have entered into their (Old Testament people's) labors. When laborers who worked in the vineyard said that these last men have worked only one hour, and you made them equal to us who have borne the burden and the heat of the day."

Jesus said, "I say to you that many prophets and righteous men desired to see what you see, and did not see it, and to hear what you hear, and did not hear it." Because the one born of the Spirit is spirit. God is a Spirit and so whoever is born of the Spirit can see the kingdom of God and can see God. Jesus said that, among those born of women, there is not a greater prophet than John the Baptist; but, he, who is least in the kingdom of God, is greater than he. The least in New Testament time who has faith in Jesus is greater than John the Baptist. The physical temple that has become a den of thieves, if you destroy it, in three days I will raise it up means dying to flesh and rising in spirit.

Jesus opened the womb and was firstborn, seated at the right hand of the Father because He died in the flesh and was raised in Spirit. When Jesus took baptism, heaven opened, meaning He was buried in the flesh and raised in the Spirit. Thus, He became the firstborn of the Spirit and opened the way for us that, by the faith in His name, we can become heirs of heaven. Holy Scriptures bear witness about these things. Moses also bears witness about Him.

When the Pharisees brought a woman caught in the adultery and said that Moses, in the law, commanded us that such should be stoned, Jesus said that they judge according to the flesh.

Scripture says, "If the ministry of death, written and engraved on stones, was glorious, so that the children of Israel could not look steadily at the face of Moses because of the glory of his countenance, which glory was passing away, how will the ministry of the Spirit not be more glorious?" (2 Corinthians 3:7–8). The ministry is more glorious because of what was passing away was glorious, then how much more the ministry that was everlasting? That is more glorious!

"Who also made us sufficient as ministers of the new covenant, not of the letter but of the Spirit; for the letter kills, but the Spirit gives life." (2 Corinthians 3:6)

"He takes away the first that He may establish the second. By that will we have been sanctified through the offering of the body of Jesus Christ once for all" (Hebrews 10:9–10). The old nature is ready to vanish away. Old nature vanishes away because we walk by the Spirit and not by the flesh. By renewing our minds, we become new Earth and new heaven. Scripture says, "Unlike Moses, who put a veil over his face so that the children of Israel could not look steadily at the end of what was passing away. But their minds were blinded. For until this day the same veil remains unlifted in the reading of the Old Testament, because the veil is taken away in Christ" (2 Corinthians 3:13–14).

Thus, our physical body that lusts after the flesh is a veil or a curtain so that we cannot see God. But Jesus Christ took our sins upon Himself and suffered death for us and, with His own blood, went through the veil in the Most Holy place. Therefore, that veil is removed through Jesus Christ so that we can see God.

Scriptures say that whoever sees God, cannot live; so, as we see God, we die to the evil works of the flesh. When we completely die to the evil works of the flesh, then, by the grace of God, we can clearly see the face of God and see how God is.

Jesus fulfilled the law in His flesh and, by not committing even one sin, He destroyed sin. God punished the sin in His body. He suffered God's wrath because of us. He drank the cup of God's wrath. He fulfilled the law by obedience and established the law. Thus, by our faith in Jesus, we put on Jesus. Whatever He did, it was done for us so we can have everlasting and abundant life for free for which Jesus paid the price. So, we are free, whom the son sets free is free indeed. Whoever is born of God, does not sin. If we are one with God, we cannot sin because God is a Spirit. God is Holy and He is not according to the flesh and so we cannot sin.

SIX

NATION OF ISRAEL

51. Ground (Land)

Adam ate the fruit of the knowledge of good and evil from his wife and the ground was cursed mean death came on the ground (Earth) and Death reigned on the physical body.

Cain killed his brother Abel. God said to Cain, "The voice of your brother's blood cries out to Me from the ground. So now you are cursed from the Earth, which has opened its mouth to receive your brother's blood from your hand." With Cain who represents the physical body and Abel who represents the spiritual body, the physical body killed the spiritual body (works of God).

God said to Cain, "When you till the ground, it shall no longer yield its strength to you. A fugitive and a vagabond you shall be on the Earth" (Genesis 4:12).

When you till the ground, it shall no longer yield its strength means it will not grow any good fruit because Cain killed the works of God, and the works of the flesh are evil. Therefore, Earth will bring forth thorns and thistles for you (Cain). *Thorns* mean worldly desires, lusts, greed, and such works.

Nothing good comes from the physical body, and there is no benefit from the flesh, but the commandments Jesus gave were the good seeds by which produced the spiritual fruits that give glory to God. Every good tree (spiritual) bears good fruit, but a bad tree (physical) bears bad fruit.

In the chapter of the burning bush, God talked to Moses and sent him to free the Israelites from captivity in Egypt. *Egypt* represents the physical body and the *children of Israel* represent the spiritual body who are the heirs of the Promised Land. The physical body has enslaved the spiritual body.

God showed signs and wonders through Moses to free the children of Israel.

– Made a snake out of a stick and then a stick from the snake
– Waters became blood
– Frogs covered Egypt
– Lice on all people and animal throughout the land of Egypt
– Swarms of flies came
– Pestilence killed the livestock of Egypt
– Boils broke out on man and beast throughout Egypt
– Heavy hail killed man and beast in the field
– Locusts ate plants and trees
– There was darkness for three days

All the firstborn (physical body), from that of Pharaoh who sits on his throne to that of the female servant who is behind the handmill, were killed.

Thus, God killed the firstborn (physical body) Jesus who took our sins upon Himself. The Israelites were freed from the captivity of sin only after the firstborn son died. Thus, the children of Israel were free after 400 years of slavery. These 400 years represent 4,000 years; after that, Jesus came and freed us from the slavery of sin.

"Now the LORD had said unto Abram, Get thee out of thy country, and from thy kindred, and from thy father's house, unto a land that I will shew thee: and I will make of thee a great nation, and I will bless thee, and make thy name great; and thou shalt be a blessing." (Genesis 12:1–2 KJV)

Did God give this promise to Abraham only? This promise is also for us.

God asked Abraham to leave his country, meaning the land on which he lived, his father's house, his family and everything, and go to the land that God will show, which he will inherit, that land is flowing with milk and honey.

Abraham's country (land), which was idol worshipper, that land represents Abraham's soul. That soul lusts after all kinds of sins and becomes subject to it and worships the devil, bows down to him. Abraham left that country to inherit the Promised Land. Thus, Abraham gave up his sins and decided to walk by God's promises. This is how we are travelers on this Earth.

Abraham was childless, meaning he was not bearing any fruits for God. The way the fig tree didn't have any fruit, it was barren. Even then, God gave a promise to him that the one that will come from your own body shall be your heir. "And he brought him forth abroad, and said, Look now toward heaven, and tell the stars, if thou be able to number them: and he said unto him, So shall thy seed be" (Genesis 15:5 KJV).

Ishmael, who was born to Abraham through Hagar, a bondwoman, represents the physical body. He will not inherit the kingdom of God because it's for a short time, but in Isaac his seed shall be called who is spiritual, he will inherit the kingdom of God. God is our inheritance.

"And God gave him no inheritance in it, not even enough to set his foot on. But even when Abraham had no child, He promised to give it (the land) to him for a possession, and to his descendants after him." (Acts 7:5)

Scriptures say Abraham believed in God, and it was accounted to him for righteousness, meaning, whoever trusts in Jesus, they are descendants of Abraham. For he is not a Jew who is one outwardly but the one who also walks in the steps of the faith as Abraham had, they are the descendants of Abraham. If we are the descendants of Abraham, then we are heirs according to the promise.

When God freed the Israelites from captivity in Egypt, "The children of Israel had done according to the word of Moses, and they had asked the Egyptians articles of silver, articles of gold, and clothing. And the Lord had given the people favor in the sight of the Egyptians, so that they granted them what they requested. Thus, they plundered the Egyptians" (Exodus 12:35–36).

The wealth the Israelites received from the Egyptians was the wealth which was the wages of the slavery of sin. It was the wealth of sin.

We give our wealth of sin to Jesus and make Jesus rich related to sin. The way the rich man was able to see Lazarus and Abraham when he was in the place of torment. That rich man represents Jesus who took our sins upon Himself and suffered death.

Luke 16:1–13—The Parable of the Unjust Steward Explanation

A certain rich man represents God the Father. A steward represents us, on whom an accusation was made that this man is wasting the rich man's goods.

God the Father has given us this life, it is God's deposit, but we have wasted it in sin and prodigal living. This life is not our own, it's debt to us. When the steward was asked to give an account by the rich man, he called his debtors and wrote down the amounts they owed, so that when he is put out of the stewardship, those debtors may receive him into their houses. The steward had dealt shrewdly.

Jesus said, "And I say to you, make friends for yourselves by unrighteous mammon, that when you fail, they may receive you into an everlasting home." The *unrighteous mammon* means the wealth of sin that we earned on this Earth. We give that to poor

(Jesus) and make friends for ourselves, so that when our life is over on this Earth, our wealth is completely gone. Then, your friends will receive you into an everlasting life (tabernacle) home and you will take part in the everlasting life. You cannot serve God and mammon, so serve God only.

God promised to give the land (country) to the children of Israel, the descendants of Abraham, and they started their journey to go to the Promised Land under the leadership of Moses. Moses parted the sea and the cloud overshadowed them. They walked on dry land in the midst of the sea, became followers of Moses and, like this, were baptized into Moses. They were given the law and they started obeying the law. But, in the wilderness, they asked for meat to eat, meaning they asked to fulfill the lust of the flesh and to sin. They wanted to go back to the slavery of sin from where God had freed them, and the wrath of God was kindled against those who were disobedient. Thus, because of their unbelief and disobedience, they died in the wilderness. They could not enter the Promised Land.

The Promised Land, the country of Canaan, was a land flowing with milk and honey. *Milk,* meaning the Word of God, and *honey,* meaning the revelation of God. The Israelites could not enter that land because of their unbelief, but their children were able to enter the Promised Land. The children are those who were obedient to God, obedient to the law, submissive to God, in which were Joshua and Caleb, who loved God.

When the children of Israel, the whole congregation, under Moses' leadership came into the wilderness of Zin and stayed in Kadesh, there was no water to drink, and the people gathered against and contended with Moses and Aaron. And God said to Moses to take the rod and, with Aaron, gather the congregation together and speak to the rock before their eyes, and it will yield its water. Thus, you shall bring water for them out of the rock and give drink to the congregation and their animals.

But Moses lifted his hand and struck the rock twice with his rod; and water came out abundantly.

Moses represents Jesus, and the rock represents Jesus' soul. Moses (Jesus) struck the rock, His soul, twice representing Jesus' death on the cross. By doing this, Jesus struck His own soul. He took our sins upon Himself and sacrificed His life. And the water came out abundantly.

Paul writes, "All drank the same spiritual drink. For they drank of that spiritual Rock that followed them, and that Rock was Christ (1 Corinthians 10:4).

When Jesus took our sins upon Himself and died, the water of life came out. Jesus said, "Whoever drinks of the water that I shall give him will never thirst" (John 4:14). "He who believes in Me, as the Scripture has said, out of his heart will flow rivers of living water" (John 7:38).

Moses struck the rock so God said, "You shall see the land before you, though you shall not go there."

When the children of Israel made a molded image and turned aside from the way, God's wrath was kindled against them and He said to Moses, "Let Me alone, that I may destroy them, and blot out their name from under heaven: and I will make of thee a nation mightier and greater than they" (Deuteronomy 9:14 KJV).

Moses (Jesus) said, "Yet now, if thou wilt forgive their sin—; and if not, blot me, I pray thee, out of thy book which thou hast written" (Exodus 32:32 KJV).

And God blotted out Jesus' name from His Book of Life. Jesus took our sins upon Himself, and God blotted out Jesus' name from the Book of Life and threw him down into the Hades.

In the Parable of Lazarus and the Rich Man, Jesus represents the rich man whose name was blotted out from the Book of Life. The way God had told Moses that you will see the land before you but will not enter it. Thus, the rich man (Jesus) was able to see Abraham and Lazarus in his bosom from afar but could not go there. Thus, Jesus was separated from God the Father.

And the Lord spoke to Moses, "Send men to spy out the land of Canaan, which I am giving to the children of Israel." So, Moses sent spies to search out the land. The spies returned and informed that we went to the land where you sent us. It truly flows with milk and honey, and this is its fruit. Nevertheless, the people who dwell in the land are strong, the cities are fortified and very large, moreover, we saw the descendants of Anak there. The descendants of Anak that are strong giants, and they represent our evil thoughts, and they keep us captive in sins and rule over us. They have possessed us.

Joshua represents Jesus who fought the war to win the Promised Land. *Joshua* means "God is deliverance." Scripture says, "Israel listen, the Lord will fight for you."

Jesus fought that war for us and rejected all of the devil's proposals and didn't sin and destroyed sin. He obeyed all of God's commandments and established the law. Jesus said, "In the world you will have tribulation, but be of good cheer, I have overcome the world."

Thus, winning the Promised Land was like winning the battle of mind and Joshua (Jesus) by the sword of the Word of God removed those evil thoughts and established the Word of God. Paul says, "We have the mind of Christ." God rules from inside of us, Jesus is seated at the right hand of God and Jesus said, "He who overcomes I will grant to sit with Me on My throne." Paul said, "You have reigned as kings and we also might reign with you." We are no longer slave and under bondage of sin, but we are free in Christ.

After the children of Israel spied out Ai, they said that the people of Ai are few so let not all the people go to fight. But the children of Israel were defeated against the people of Ai, they fled before the men of Ai and thirty-six men were killed. The hearts of the people of Israel melted and become like water due to this incident.

When Achan committed sin regarding accursed things, Joshua prayed and God said that Israel has sinned, and they have also transgressed God's covenant which God commanded them. For they have even taken some of the accursed things and have both stolen and deceived. Then Achan was caught and Joshua, and all of Israel with him, took Achan the son of Zerah, the silver, the garment, the wedge of gold, his sons, his daughters, his oxen, his donkeys, his sheep, his tent, and all that he had, and they brought them to the Valley of Achor and stoned him with stones and burned them with fire. They raised over him a great heap of stones, still there to this day.

Thus, all the sins that are in us such as theft, fornication, jealousies, drunkenness, lusts, revelries, we should destroy them by stoning means by the law and burn them with fire means destroy by the fire of the Holy Spirit.

We compare the evil thoughts of the lust of the flesh with the serpent. They represent the serpent and the seed of the serpent, and we should destroy them by the stone (the law). We should crush the head of the serpent (sin) and remove the thought of sin. Thus, remove the evil from among us. That represents Achan, his wife, and children.

Joshua (Jesus) won most of the Promised Land and he was advanced in age. He gained a lot of experience in war and became mature. After he died, the rest of the land was won in battle by the children of Israel that represent those who are to be firstfruits with Jesus. Thus, they received the Promised Land.

Explanation of the Parable of the Sower

When someone hears the word of the kingdom and does not understand it, then the wicked one comes and snatches away what was sown in his heart. This is he who received seed by the wayside. Scripture says, "Too much eating and drinking causes the heart to be stubborn like stone." Too much consumption of sin causes stubbornness of mind. He does not accept the word because he doesn't have any value of it.

He who received the seed on stony places, this is he who hears the word and immediately receives it with joy, yet he has no root in himself, but endures only for a while. For when tribulation or persecution arises because of the word, immediately he stumbles. This means after repenting and leaving sin, he has to endure the suffering that comes with walking in God's ways and with the renewing of mind; struggles and temptations come, but he sees all these and he goes back to the old life.

And he who received seed among the thorns is he who hears the word, and the cares of this world, and the deceitfulness of riches choke the word. This means the flesh, which is equal to thorns; it chokes the word out due to the lust of the flesh and all kinds of sins and stops the seed to grow.

Thus, due to the lust of the flesh, we cannot bear fruit for God. But, if we destroy the evil works of the flesh by the Spirit, remove the stubbornness which is like stone and the covetousness of wealth which is like a thorn, then the ground will be fruitful for us, and we can bear 100% fruits for God by the grace of Jesus Christ.

Thus, some bear fruit and produce a hundredfold, some sixty and some thirty.

As much as we gain God on this Earth, that much we will receive Him in the new life in the resurrection.

When Israelites were in slavery (sins) in Egypt, God sent Moses and killing the firstborn (Jesus) of Egypt, freed Israelites from slavery. Thus, the Israelites who represent woman was redeemed by blood then the exodus happened from Egypt. On the way, the sea was parted meaning the water above (spiritual) and water below (physical) were separated and brought them to the desert.

Moses was leading the Israelites. Moses represents Jesus, who is a good shepherd. To guide the Israelites, there was pillar of cloud during the day and the pillar of fire during the night. That pillar represents the Holy Spirit who leads us in all truth and righteousness and helps us to walk in the way.

When they were in the desert, they asked for meat which represents the lust of the flesh. Therefore, they died in the desert because of their unbelief but those who resisted temptation and were successful reached to the Promised Land. They became the bride that was without wrinkle and blemish and lived in the Promised Land.

Those who kept themselves holy in the Promised Land represents the bride who will marry Christ and they will become one.

52. Earth Is Hell

Heaven is His throne, and Earth is His footstool. There is darkness under His feet.

"And the Earth was without form, and void; and darkness was upon the face of the deep. And the Spirit of God moved upon the face of the waters." (Genesis 1:2 KJV)

Earth represents our soul as well as our Promised Land. We are made of dirt. Everyone is an Earth in itself. Mark writes, "For what will it profit a man if he gains the whole world, and loses his own soul?" (Mark 8:36). Thus, our soul is compared to Earth. So, if we, by the lust of the flesh, fulfill our worldly desires and live in pleasure and lose our soul, what profit is there? We will be separated from God for eternity. What will we profit when we lose our soul?

Each person is Earth in itself, and we are separated from God because of sin, therefore, Earth is hell. We are without form, and void; and darkness is on the face of the deep. The god of the world has blinded us relative to God. Jesus said, "If the blind leads the blind, both will fall into a ditch." There was light (God) in Jesus and that light was life for mankind.

In the land of Zebulun and the land of Naphtali, by the way of the sea, beyond the Jordan, in Galilee of the Gentiles, the people who walked in darkness have seen a great light; those who dwelt in the land of the shadow of death, upon them a light (Jesus) had shined.

To live separated from God is to live in hell. John the Baptist said, "And even now the ax is laid to the root of the trees. Therefore, every tree which does not bear good fruit is cut down and thrown into the fire" (Matthew 3:10). *Tree* represents life of mankind and they are sent on this Earth on a journey. Each tree that does not bear good fruit is cut down and thrown into the fire. This fire is separation from God for eternity. "Blessed are the meek, for they shall inherit the Earth" (Matthew 5:5). The one who obeys God's commandments is the one who humbles himself under God and inherits the Earth means will receive abundant life.

Jesus took our sins upon Himself on the cross and said, "My God, My God, why have you forsaken me?" God leaves Jesus because of sin and darkness falls upon Jesus. Darkness stayed for three hours. God placed man on the Earth to rule over the Earth but, by sinning against God, he brought darkness, death, upon himself. Jesus said, "Do not think that I came to bring peace on Earth. I did not come to bring peace but a sword" (Matthew 10:34). When the light of Jesus shines on us, we can see our sins and the works of darkness within us. Then, the war breaks through within us. The flesh wars against the spirit and the spirit wars against the flesh.

Paul says, "You have not yet resisted to bloodshed, striving against sin" (Romans 12:4). This means you have not yet destroyed the works of the flesh through the sword of the word. Scriptures say, "Moon became blood." This *moon* means the believers who, through spiritual warfare, destroys sin and the moon tuned into blood. The sun's (Jesus') light shines on the moon and the wicked works are revealed. Thus, Jesus separates light from darkness as in the creation God caused a firmament in the midst of the waters and divided the waters from the waters. So, God organized the Earth that was without form. God said to not be unequally yoked together with unbelievers. If you marry, marry believers.

Paul said, "What communion has light with darkness?" In the same way, what communion has holiness with sin? They both are against each other. There is a war between the flesh and the spirit. We must war against the works of the flesh by the Spirit and inherit the Earth.

When we were deep in sin and darkness, Jesus came into our lives as the light. When we saw the works of the darkness within us, we repented and destroyed our sinful works. After that, we walk after Jesus who is the light and become children of the light.

God has planted us on this Earth and gave us life so that we can bear good fruits for God and give glory to God. We should give glory to God with our bodies. God has given us this life, so our lives are His wealth. If you have not been faithful in what belongs to another, who will give you what is your own? So, if we are a faithful servant to God, one day, a dear servant of the master will become His son.

Scriptures says, "The time of the dead has come, that they should be judged, and should destroy those who destroy the Earth" (Revelation 11:18). This body represents Earth. If we misuse the freedom that God has given us and live according to our own will, we bring destruction to ourselves. Thus, we lose our lives. So, we should give our bodies as instruments to God. We should bring them in the temple of God for use as there are vessels of many kinds in the temple. We should become the kind of vessels that is used for the great purpose of God.

53. Belly

When the woman ate the forbidden fruit, the Lord God said to the woman, "What is this you have done?" The woman said, "The serpent deceived me, and I ate." So, the Lord God said to the serpent, "Because you have done this, you are cursed more than all cattle, and more than every beast of the field. On your belly you shall go, and you shall eat dust all the days of your life and I will put enmity between you and the woman, and between your seed and her Seed. He shall bruise your head, and you shall bruise His heel."

God created Adam and Eve to exercise authority over Earth and to rule over all animals. But the serpent that is the devil that deceived the woman and, due to disobedience to God, the devil took authority over them. This means the physical body that Adam and Eve were supposed to rule became ruler over them. Thus, Adam and Eve became slave to sin, and the devil was their ruler. By doing this, their lives became upside down, meaning the physical body ruled and the spiritual body was under feet.

Serpent means a thought which is lust of the flesh. The commandment was not to fulfill that lust of the flesh; do not put that thought (sin) in action. But Eve fulfilled her thought and sinned.

The Lord God said to the serpent: "Because you have done this, you are cursed more than all cattle, and more than every beast of the field; On your belly you shall go, and you shall eat dust all the days of your life." This means all the evil thoughts are the lusts of the flesh and they are lusts of our belly. We fulfill the lusts of our bellies, and we walk according to that. Scriptures say that the enemies of the cross of Christ, whose end is destruction, whose god is their belly, meaning they walk according to the lust of the flesh and bow down to it. The way every sin is equal to idol worship, they bow down to sin and become slaves of sin.

The butler and the baker are two kinds of services. Offering service represents the butler, who offers himself as living sacrifice that is pleasing to God. The second service of the baker means serving the belly that fulfills the lust of the flesh. Thus, God said to the serpent (thought of lust of the flesh), "You shall eat dust all the days of your life," meaning you will fulfill the lust of the flesh.

"For our soul is bowed down to the dust: Our belly cleaveth unto the Earth. Arise for our help, And redeem us for thy mercies' sake." (Psalm 44:25–26 KJV)

The leech has two daughters—
Give and Give!
There are three *things* that are never satisfied,
Four never say, "Enough!":
The grave,
The barren womb,
The Earth *that* is not satisfied with water—
And the fire never says, "Enough!" (Proverbs 30:15–16)

Thus, the things that are never satisfied are barren womb (belly or Sheol). Our lusts of the flesh, hunger, and wishes, they never say enough and never satisfy. The earth that is not satisfied with water, meaning the earth that absorbs water that falls frequently, which despises the grace of God, and the fire that never says enough, no matter how much fuel you add, they never say enough.

"Like sheep they are laid in the grave; Death shall feed on them; And the upright shall have dominion over them in the morning; And their beauty shall consume in the grave from their dwelling." (Psalm 49:14 KJV)

Fish represents the soul that lusts after the flesh. Jesus said, "No sign will be given to it except the sign of the prophet Jonah." When Jesus took our sins upon Himself on the cross, God prepared a great fish to swallow Jonah (Jesus) and he was in the belly of the fish for three days and three nights. Then Jonah

(Jesus) prayed to the Lord from the fish's belly. He said, "I cried out to the Lord because of my affliction, and He answered me, out of the belly of Sheol I cried and He heard my voice."

Jonah (Jesus) was in the belly of the fish for three days and three nights means he was in the belly of Sheol for 3,000 years and went down to the depth of the Sheol. He proclaimed liberty to the captives and freed them, Jesus went down to the depth of the Sheol means He came down in the midst of us. We live in Sheol, separated from God in darkness, we forgot God, dip down in sin, and Jesus said, "So ought not this woman, being a daughter of Abraham, whom Satan has bound—think of it—for eighteen years, be loosed from this bond on the Sabbath?"(Luke 13:16). *Sabbath* means the seventh day for the slave to be free. On this day, each male and female slave is set free; this is the year of freedom. Thus, He preached the Gospel and set the captives free.

"For in death there is no remembrance of thee: In the grave who shall give thee thanks?" (Psalm 6:5 KJV)

Death means die out to the works of God and walk according to the works of the flesh. On that stage, we do not remember God nor worship Him because evildoers forget God. So, they become strangers to God, who do not know God. Scriptures say that evil doers are lazy gluttons, meaning they fulfill the lust of the flesh, but Jesus prayed from the belly of Sheol, and God heard His prayer. Jesus said, "Father, I know that you always hear me," and then He raised Lazarus from the dead means we who are captives will rise on the fourth day which is in fourth millennium AD during 8000s with Jesus to be firstfruits with Him.

Those who die to the works of the flesh, to them Jesus said, "The water that I shall give him will become in him a fountain of water springing up into everlasting life" (John 4:14).

The belly, which is the Sheol, if we stop the lusts of the flesh, living water will flow from it. Jesus said that I have the keys of

Hades and *of Death* and the power of hell (Sheol/Hades) will not prevail against the church.

54. Garden of Eden

Eden means a place of happiness where Adam and Eve lived in glory with God. God lived with them. They lived inside of God and God lived in them; that's how they lived. Earth represents us; each individual person is Earth in itself. In the midst of the Garden of Eden, God created the tree of life and the tree of the knowledge of good and evil.

The *tree of the knowledge of good and evil* means a physical body and the *tree of life* is the spiritual body. God commanded that we should not eat of the tree of good and evil meaning we should not fulfill the lust of the flesh but live by the Spirit. They were one with God in Spirit and they were immortal, meaning they would never die.

But the woman ate of the tree of the knowledge of good and evil, experiencing sin, brought death upon herself and became mortal. The wages of sin is death, so death came on her body, and it became mortal.

"And the LORD God said, Behold, the man is become as one of us, to know good and evil: and now, lest he put forth his hand, and take also of the tree of life, and eat, and live for ever: therefore the LORD God sent him forth from the garden of Eden, to till the ground from whence he was taken" (Genesis 3:22–23 KJV). God said to Cain that when he tills the ground, it will no longer yield its strength to him. He will be a fugitive and a vagabond on the Earth. Cain killed his brother Abel (spiritual), so he was separated from God and so the ground was cursed and it will not give its strength.

God is a Spirit and, because of sin, God was separated from mankind. The glory mankind was experiencing with God, they lost that glory. And Adam said that I was afraid because I was naked, and I hid myself. Thus, being separated from God, we become naked and full of darkness. In the darkness of hell, everyone is naked and exposed. God is light and when Adam was separated from God because of sin, he was filled with darkness which is death. God departed from him, and the Garden of Eden was no longer a place of happiness. In God, there is love, joy, peace, and abundant life and there is no death or darkness.

"So he drove out the man; and he placed at the east of the garden of Eden Cherubims, and a flaming sword which turned every way, to keep the way of the tree of life." (Genesis 3:24 KJV)

This tree of life is Jesus and so, to guard the way to the tree of life that no one can eat that fruit, God placed a flaming sword which turned every way, as God is a consuming fire. Jesus is the second Adam, God lived in Him, and Jesus was experiencing Glory with God.

"To him who overcomes I will give to eat from the tree of life, which is in the midst of the Paradise of God." (Revelation 2:7)

Whoever says no to darkness and yes to the light and glorifying God lasts until the end, to him God will give the fruit of life from the midst of Paradise to eat, meaning the eternal life as inheritance and God will be his heritage.

In the burning bush chapter, when Moses goes near the burning bush, the Lord said to Moses not to draw near the place and to take his sandals off his feet, for the place where he stood was holy ground. Moreover, God said that He is the God of his father—the God of Abraham, the God of Isaac, and the God of Jacob. So, if we seek God, He is not far from any of us. Moses sought the Lord and he found Him.

That burning bush was Jesus; God lived inside of Jesus and Jesus lived inside of God. Jesus had a glorified body. Jesus left all the glory that He had with God and became zero and came down to this Earth. Leaving immortal glorified body, He became mortal being in the likeness of a sinful flesh. The way children are of the flesh and the blood, He came in the same way. To save us, He stepped down into the darkness.

Jesus said, "When they persecute you in this city, flee to another. For assuredly, I say to you, you will not have gone through the cities of Israel before the Son of Man comes." We are Earth itself and, after receiving Jesus Christ, we preach the Gospel within ourselves and all in our household get saved and, before we go through all the cities, Jesus returns in our lives. The way Moses lived in Midian for forty years and preached and reached the place where God was at the burning bush. As on this Earth, God is only in Israel and we need to reach there. He is not far from any of us. He is inside of us.

55. Wrath of God

"But when he saw many of the Pharisees and Sadducees coming to his baptism, he said to them, 'Brood of vipers! Who warned you to flee from the wrath to come?'" (Matthew 3:7)

So, the wrath of God will come upon those who are disobedient. The way God brought plagues on Egypt, but God told the Israelites, "If you obey my commandments, none of the plagues will come upon you."

"He who believes in the Son has everlasting life; and he who does not believe the Son shall not see life, but the wrath of God abides on him" (John 3:36). The Son that is Jesus and those who believe in Him means those who obey His commandments will have eternal life, but those who do not believe, God's wrath comes upon them.

"But in accordance with your hardness and your impenitent heart you are treasuring up for yourself wrath in the day of wrath and revelation of the righteous judgment of God, who will render to each one according to his deeds" (Romans 2:5–6). When Jesus comes, He will give each according to the works of his hands and they will be separated from God forever. Thus, the wrath of God will be poured out.

"What if God, wanting to show His wrath and to make His power known, endured with much long-suffering the vessels of wrath prepared for destruction?" (Romans 9:22)

"Among whom also we all once conducted ourselves in the lusts of our flesh, fulfilling the desires of the flesh and of the mind, and were by nature children of wrath, just as the others." (Ephesians 2:3)

"And the kings of the Earth, the great men, the rich men, the commanders, the mighty men, every slave and every free man, hid themselves in the caves and in the rocks of the mountains, and said to the mountains and rocks, 'Fall on us and hide us from the face of Him who sits on the throne and from the wrath of the Lamb! For the great day of His wrath has come, and who is able to stand?'" (Revelation 6:15–17)

Evil will not be able to stand before the throne because the day of the judgment has come on those who are disobedient. "Then I heard a loud voice from the temple saying to the seven angels, 'Go and pour out the bowls of the wrath of God on the Earth'" (Revelation 16:1). This means those who had the mark of the beast, and those who worshipped the beast, bowed down to him and were submitted to him; on those, the wrath of God was poured out.

But those who have accepted Jesus as their Lord and Savior and have faith in Him, the blood of Jesus was put on their heads. The way when the firstborns of Egypt were killed, the Israelites put the blood on their doorposts and the angel of death didn't kill them in the same way those who believe in Jesus will be saved from the wrath of God.

We are under the grace of our Lord Jesus and His blood covers all our sins. He does not impute sin to us that is His grace. We should not abuse His grace, but we should abide in Him. In Christ, we are a holy nation, a holy people, and priests to God and kings.

56. Seed of a Woman

> And the LORD God said unto the woman, What is this that thou hast done? And the woman said, The serpent beguiled me, and I did eat. And the LORD God said unto the serpent, Because thou hast done this, thou art cursed above all cattle, and above every beast of the field; upon thy belly shalt thou go, and dust shalt thou eat all the days of thy life: and I will put enmity between thee and the woman, and between thy seed and her seed; it shall bruise thy head, and thou shalt bruise his heel. (Genesis 3:13–15 KJV)

Serpent means a thought of lust of the physical body which the woman listened to and carried out the thought and sinned and became a slave to sin. Thus, God said to the serpent, "You are cursed more than all cattle and every beast of the field," meaning death will reign on you and on your belly; you shall go, meaning you will walk according to the lust of the flesh and eat dust all the days of your life, which means fulfill the lust of the flesh. "And I will put enmity between you and the woman and between your seed and her seed," meaning woman and her offspring (seed) and enmity between your seed, and her seed means enmity between the physical body and the spiritual body. Destroy the works of the flesh with the Spirit.

Woman's Seed shall bruise your head and you shall bruise His heel. Woman's Seed that is Jesus who was born of a virgin, and He crushed the devil's head and woman has that Seed in her.

"And God said, Let the Earth bring forth grass, the herb yielding seed, and the fruit tree yielding fruit after his kind, whose seed is in itself, upon the Earth: and it was so" (Genesis 1:11 KJV). Jesus' seed was already in us as the virgin shall be with child and bear a Son.

"Remember that Jesus Christ, of the seed of David, was raised from the dead according to my Gospel." (2 Timothy 2:8)

"Having been born again, not of corruptible seed but incorruptible, through the Word of God which lives and abides forever." (1 Peter 1:23)

If God had not kept His (Jesus') Seed in us, we would have perished a long time ago, but because God kept Him for us so that whoever believes in Him would not perish but have eternal life.

"Who hath believed our report? and to whom is the arm of the LORD revealed? For he shall grow up before him as a tender plant, and as a root out of a dry ground: he hath no form nor comeliness; and when we shall see him, there is no beauty that we should desire him" (Isaiah 53:1–2 KJV). That Jesus the Son of God, who as a root out of dry ground, was born on this Earth.

The Son of Man (Jesus) sows good seed which is spiritual so that we can bring forth spiritual fruits and glorify God.

"Again, the kingdom of heaven is like treasure hidden in a field, which a man found and hid; and for joy over it he goes and sells all that he has and buys that field." (Matthew 13:44)

Paul said, "Seek the Lord, in the hope that you might grope for Him and find Him, though He is not far from each one of us. Paul is saying that He was already in us as a hidden treasure in a vessel of dirt.

The field is us and Jesus was already in us who is a treasure. He was found by a man and then that man sold everything means he gave up all his wealth of sin and bought that field and received treasure, meaning he received Jesus in his life. He found and hid means he kept his life a secret before God and gave up all his sins that was his wealth and bought a field in which was a treasure, and that treasure was Jesus Christ. There was life in Jesus and that life was the light of men.

"Again, the kingdom of heaven is like a merchant seeking beautiful pearls, who, when he had found one pearl of great price, went and sold all that he had and bought it." (Matthew 13:45–46)

The one pearl of great price is Jesus Christ, and we are the merchant who was seeking for beautiful pearls. He sold all that he had, that are all sins and bought the pearl. Jesus said, "Ask, and it will be given to you; seek, and you will find; knock, and it will be opened to you" (Matthew 7:7). Thus, if we ask for the Holy Spirit, we will receive; if we seek the kingdom of God, we will find it; and, if we knock on the door of God's heart, it will be opened to us.

He was already in us. Jesus said that he who overcomes I will give to eat from the tree of life, which is in the midst of the Paradise of God.

57. Adam's Helper

"And the Lord God said, "It is not good that man should be alone; I will make him a helper comparable to him." (Genesis 2:18)

Adam is Jesus.

"And the LORD God caused a deep sleep to fall upon Adam, and he slept: and he took one of his ribs, and closed up the flesh instead thereof; and the rib, which the LORD God had taken from man, made he a woman, and brought her unto the man. And Adam said, This is now bone of my bones, and flesh of my flesh: she shall be called Woman, because she was taken out of Man." (Genesis 2:21–23 KJV)

Scripture says, "Another parable He put forth to them, saying: 'The kingdom of heaven is like a man who sowed good seed in his field; but while men slept, his enemy came and sowed tares among the wheat and went his way'" (Matthew 13:24–25).

When Jesus was crucified and there was darkness from the sixth hour until the ninth hour, and tares that represent our sins, Jesus took them on Himself. At that time, God created woman out of Jesus. "And Jesus said, 'The glory which You gave Me I have given them, that they may be one just as We are one'" (John 17:22).

Jesus took our darkness (sins) and gave us His glory. Thus, we received new birth through Him. He redeemed us by His blood. We were called *woman* because we were taken out of Man. Jesus said, "See that a spirit does not have flesh and bones as you see I have." The way Adam said, this is now bone of my bones and flesh of my flesh. In which there is no blood, there is life in the blood, and it lusts after sin. We became spiritual through Jesus. He sowed good seed in us, He gave us commandments. The spiritual is not first, but the natural (physical) and, afterward, the spiritual.

Jesus gave His own life for us. The bride of Christ who is prepared to marry Jesus, she dies to the works of the flesh and lives according to the Spirit. She gives her life for Jesus and proves her love for Christ. God gives her opportunity to prove her love for Christ. There is no greater love than this to lay down one's life for his friends (John 15:13). The bride sacrifices herself for Christ.

Matthew 22:1–14—The Parable of the Wedding Feast Explanation

The kingdom of heaven is like a certain king who arranged a marriage for his son. The *King* represents God the Father and the *Son* is Jesus Christ. Guests were invited to the wedding feast. While the King came to see the guests, he saw a man who did not have the wedding garments on, meaning he was naked. He did not have the works of God in him. Scripture says, "In Sheol, they are naked and exposed." Obedience covers our nakedness. Jesus' blood covers our nakedness. We should put on Jesus. So, we should walk worthy of the calling which we were called, so that we may be accepted and counted worthy of the kingdom of God.

58. White Dove's Vision

One morning, I was cleaning my kitchen counter and the Holy Spirit talked to me, "Why aren't you doing three days fasting . . . ?" After that, I started three days of fasting and, I was thinking, God will give me something for fasting these three days. After three days of fasting, on the fourth day, I was sleeping in the afternoon, and I sat up in my spirit and I saw a glorious white Dove in my room. It was flying around in my room. There was bright white light coming out of it, that kind of white color I have never seen on this Earth. After that, it started to go somewhere else, and I also went after it in the spirit. It took me to where Benny Hinn's crusade was going on. I saw Benny Hinn there and people worshiping God. The whole stadium was filled with people. I saw all that and immediately I was back in my body. This vision happened about ten years ago. When God asked me to write this book, the Holy Spirit reminded me of this vision and said, "If you will follow after me, I will give you this kind of ministry." I told the Lord, "I have not come straight after you. I have made many mistakes in my walking after you. I have done many foolish things and many sins." The Holy Spirit said, "All of that will not be counted against you because of the blood of Jesus."

Jesus' blood covers our sins and we are under His hand of grace.

After few days of this conversation, I had a dream. I saw a dead man on a stretcher in a hospital. He was covered with a shroud from head to toe, and the Holy Spirit was standing next to him. The Holy Spirit said, "I have given you a ministry to raise the dead," meaning the ministry of resurrection. From now on, people will hear the word of the Son of God and the dead will rise. After that, my dream ended and I was very happy that God has given me a ministry to serve.

59. New Creation

We are a new creation in Christ Jesus. *New Earth* means us, and *new heaven* means Jesus Christ.

"He will be great and will be called the Son of the Highest; and the Lord God will give Him the throne of His father David. And He will reign over the house of Jacob forever, and of His kingdom there will be no end." (Luke 1:32–33)

When Jesus appears in our lives, He establishes His Kingdom. He sits in the temple as God. He is the King forever. God the Father has made Him equal to Himself and He is seated at the right hand of God. And whoever wins, Jesus will also let him sit on His throne.

In the beginning, God created the heavens and the Earth. God created us in perfect form, but in the second verse, it says, "The Earth was formless and empty, and darkness covered the deep waters." Thus, the devil made our life formless and brought us in the bondage of darkness. And God sent Jesus Christ on this Earth and people saw the light. Jesus gave His commandments and separated light from darkness. Thus, we were separated from the darkness and through the word, we started war with the darkness. The flesh and the Spirit became contrary to each other. "And God said, Let the waters under the heaven be gathered together unto one place, and let the dry land appear: and it was so" (Genesis 1:9 KJV). "And the Earth brought forth grass, and herb yielding seed after his kind, and the tree yielding fruit, whose seed was in itself, after his kind: and God saw that it was good." (Genesis 1:12 KJV). Thus, His seed was already in us.

The larger light is the *sun,* which represents Jesus, which was created on the fourth day. The larger light to govern the day, and the smaller one to govern the night, God also made the stars. The moon that represents the nation of Israel to whom God gave the law and the sun shined on the moon. The moon does not have its own light.

Thus, God created mankind to rule the Earth. Jesus took our sins upon Himself and reconciled us with God. Thus, God created mankind in His own image, and He created them man and woman. Thus, Jesus made mankind complete and the heavens and the Earth, and all the host of them, were finished. Jesus on the cross knowing that all have completed said, "It is finished," and bowed His head and gave up his soul.

Therefore, in Christ Jesus, we are a new creation, and He is our Father. By Him we are born again. We were born of the Spirit.

"Then He who sat on the throne said, 'Behold, I make all things new.' And He said to me, 'Write, for these words are true and faithful.'" (Revelation 21:5)

"Now I saw a new heaven and a new Earth, for the first heaven and the first Earth had passed away. Therefore, if anyone is in Christ, he is a new creation; old things have passed away; behold, all things have become new." (2 Corinthians 5:17)

60. Sabbath Day

"And God blessed the seventh day, and sanctified it: because that in it he had rested from all his work which God created and made." (Genesis 2:3 KJV)

And Jesus said on the cross, "It is finished," and, thus, the heavens and the Earth, and all the host of them, were finished and He made man complete.

Surely, you should keep the Sabbaths and you should not do any work on that day.

"Ye shall keep the sabbath therefore; for it is holy unto you: every one that defileth it shall surely be put to death: for whosoever doeth any work therein, that soul shall be cut off from among his people" (Exodus 31:14 KJV). This means the Sabbath belongs to God. There is no darkness in that day, but if someone still does the works of the flesh, he shall be killed and cut off from among his people because it is impossible to repent again.

"If thou buy an Hebrew servant, six years he shall serve: and in the seventh he shall go out free for nothing" (Exodus 21:2 KJV). So, the seventh year is a year of freedom.

The seventh day is God's Sabbath means the kingdom of God which is during 7000s, in which God will rule for 1,000 years. The new heaven and the new Earth where Satan will be bound for 1,000 years. The lion shall eat straw like the ox and not devour any, not eat meat, and the nursing child shall play by the cobra's hole, and the weaned child shall put his hand in the viper's den. They shall not hurt nor destroy.

Paul says that to whom did He swear that they would not enter His rest, but to those who did not obey? Because they did not obey God and for forty years tested God in the desert, He was angry with them. Those who sinned, their corpses fell in the wilderness. So, we see that they could not enter in because of unbelief.

Paul writes, "Therefore, since a promise remains of entering His rest, let us fear lest any of you seem to have come short of it" (Hebrews 4:1).

Jesus performed many miracles on the Sabbath and freed those who were bound by the devil. He performed the works, so that there would be no imperfection in anyone; the blind could see, the lame could walk, the lepers were cleansed, therefore, the kingdom of God's rest (Sabbath) means the kingdom of freedom.

As Peter asks, how often shall my brother sin against me, and I forgive him? And Jesus answered, "Up to seventy times seven."

> And thou shalt number seven sabbaths of years unto thee, seven times seven years; and the space of the seven sabbaths of years shall be unto thee forty and nine years. Then shalt thou cause the trumpet of the jubile to sound on the tenth day of the seventh month, in the day of atonement shall ye make the trumpet sound throughout all your land. And ye shall hallow the fiftieth year, and proclaim liberty throughout all the land unto all the inhabitants thereof: it shall be a jubile unto you; and ye shall return every man unto his possession, and

ye shall return every man unto his family. (Leviticus 25:8–10 KJV)

Thus, we forgive our brother seventy times seven and return to our home and free ourselves from the bondages of the devil. We can go back to our family. Thus, we become new. Jesus said, "See I make all things new, new heaven and new Earth." We are the new Earth in which there is no sea and no need for purification and *new heaven* means Jesus as God, Son of David. We are a new creation in Christ Jesus.

God's kingdom is for 1,000 years means in which there is the light of the sun, God is that light and there is no darkness in Him.

Peter writes, "And so, we have the prophetic word confirmed, which you do well to heed as a light that shines in a dark place, until the day dawns and the morning star rises in your hearts" (2 Peter 1:19). This means, until the morning star, Jesus rises in your hearts and shines as a light of the day, have faith in the prophetic word in which you have hope; until that comes to pass, be patient. Weeping may endure for a night, but joy comes in the morning. There is light in the kingdom of God and you will see clearly. Jesus leads you with His triumph.

When Joshua fought war with the Amorites and he said to the sun to stand still; it stood still for a whole day and, in the light, they won the war with the Amorites, meaning they defeated the devil. Joshua represents Jesus to whom God the Father asked why this fig tree doesn't bear any fruit and why does it use up the ground. Cut it down, Jesus asked for grace that the tree be left alone this year, and if it does not bear any fruit, then it can be cut down. Thus, Jesus asked for a year of grace, and the sun stood still, and God's kingdom of light stayed as is. Therefore, the seventh and eighth days are the days of light and there is no night, no sundown. The seventh day is during the years 7000s , the year of God's kingdom, and 8th day is during 8000s , the year for a sign of circumcision, sign of perfection, which is the day of the resurrection. New Earth and new heaven.

SEVEN

ANGEL

61. The Sign of Abomination

Abomination of desolation means son of perdition.

The woman who rebelled against God conceives sin and gives birth to son of perdition.

James says, "But each one is tempted when he is drawn away by his own desires and enticed. Then, when desire has conceived, it gives birth to sin; and sin, when it is full-grown, brings forth death" (James 1:14-15).

When someone keep rejecting God and the works of God, eventually the works of God die out completely in them and they conceive sin and give birth to sin. That sin when fully grown brings forth death.

The Scripture says, "Let no one deceive you by any means; for that Day will not come unless the falling away comes first, and the man of sin is revealed, the son of perdition who opposes and exalts himself above all that is called God or that is worshiped, so that he sits as God in the temple of God, showing himself that he is God" (2 Thessalonians 2:3-4).

"Therefore when you see the 'abomination of desolation,' spoken of by Daniel the prophet, standing in the holy place" (whoever reads, let him understand)" (Matthew 24:15).

When Jesus was tempted by the devil, devil takes Him to Jerusalem and sets Him on the pinnacle of the temple. Jesus stood on the pinnacle of the temple as God represents the son of perdition. See that abomination of desolation standing in the holy place.

Scriptures say that our body is the temple of the living God but we all have sinned drawing away by the desires of the flesh and sinned and fall short of the glory of God. Mankind whom God created out of dirt, they didn't give God place but by committing every sin which is idol worshiping, conceived and gave birth to the son of perdition. When he is fully grown, we made him god. The body that was in the image of God, we created the image of devil in that place. God's commandment was not to make for yourself an idol but we make an idol and give life to sin. Whatever is born of the flesh is flesh and carnal mind is death.

Before the son of perdition is revealed in someone's life, falling away will come meaning he will be separated from righteousness forever because God is righteous. And then the lawless one will be revealed, whom the Lord will consume with the breath of His mouth and destroy with the brightness of His coming. People who live this kind of lives will destroy their bodies and souls.

"And then the lawless one will be revealed, whom the Lord will consume with the breath of His mouth and destroy with the brightness of His coming" (2 Thessalonians 2:8).

"For there will be no prospect for the evil man; The lamp of the wicked will be put out" (Proverb 20:20).

Thus, the unrighteous will put out their lamp of the spirit.

The rebelled woman joins the husband of sin which is lust of the flesh and conceiving sin, gives birth to the son of perdition that represents multitudes of people who walk according to the flesh and preach sin. They stand against God and deceive those who dwell on the earth and blasphemy God. Those who follow them chose the broader way. They are worldly but the friendship with this world is enmity with God. So, we should not fulfill the lusts of the flesh and not worship flesh but by obeying God's commandments we should create image of God in us. God's will is that no one perishes.

Paul says, "And do not present your members as instruments of unrighteousness to sin, but present yourselves to God as being alive from the dead, and your members as instruments of righteousness to God" (Romans 6:13).

When Jesus was tempted by the devil, the tempter talked to Jesus. That devil was Jesus' physical body which lusts after the flesh, but Jesus did not fulfill any lusts of the flesh but obeyed God in everything. Scripture says, Jesus was tempted in all points as we are but He did not sin and in the same way we should also not sin.

62. Jesus Fully Revealed God

Jesus said, "Do not think that I came to bring peace on Earth. I did not come to bring peace but a sword" (Matthew 10:34).

We were one with our flesh, fulfilling the lust of the flesh, and living in sin peacefully. But Jesus, who is the light of the world, came into our lives as light and we saw the works of the darkness within us. Through Jesus, we got separated from darkness and came into the light. Jesus separated the darkness from the light. Thus, the spirit and the flesh became contrary to each other, and the war began within us.

Jesus said, "Your enemies will be those of your own household." *Your own household* means your own flesh that lusts after sin; that flesh will war against you to give up the works of God and bring death to them. Thus, our peace was broken.

Jesus was spiritual and He never lived according to the flesh, but He took our sins to save us. He sacrificed His physical body for us. If he had not taken our sins upon Himself, He would have never died. The wages of sin is death, He paid that price for us.

And God has highly exalted Jesus above all His brethren and made Him Christ and the Lord. The Lord our God, the Lord is one!

But, when He again brings the firstborn into the world, He says, "Let all the angels of God worship Him but to the Son He says: 'Your throne, O God, is forever and ever; A scepter of righteousness is the scepter of Your kingdom'" (Hebrews 1:6–8).

The Son of David will reign forever.

Jesus was also in a physical body, so I told the Lord, that I have never worshipped someone's physical body. The Lord said, "I will show you the worship of the physical body." When Daniel reveals Nebuchadnezzar's dream and interprets the dream, "Then the king Nebuchadnezzar fell upon his face, and worshipped Daniel, and commanded that they should offer an oblation and sweet odours unto him. The king answered unto Daniel, and said, Of a truth it is, that your God is a God of gods, and a Lord of kings, and a revealer of secrets, seeing thou couldest reveal this secret" (Daniel 2:46–47 KJV). The King worshipped Daniel because through him God was revealed and glorified. Daniel represents Jesus, who revealed God. He was in a physical body, but he was spiritual.

In the Book of Revelation, John writes "I saw One like the Son of Man," meaning Jesus is in the midst of the seven lampstands who is the Son of Man as God.

> And in the midst of the seven lampstands One like the Son of Man, clothed with a garment down to the feet and girded about the chest with a golden band. His head and hair were white like wool, as white as snow, and His eyes like a flame of fire; His feet were like fine brass, as if refined in a furnace, and

His voice as the sound of many waters; He had in His right hand seven stars, out of His mouth went a sharp two-edged sword, and His countenance was like the sun shining in its strength. And when I saw Him, I fell at His feet as dead. But He laid His right hand on me, saying to me, "Do not be afraid; I am the First and the Last." (Revelation 1:13–17)

He causes all, both small and great, rich and poor, free and slave, to receive a mark on their right hand or on their foreheads, and that no one may buy or sell except one who has the mark or the name of the beast, or the number of his name. Here is wisdom. Let him who has understanding calculate the number of the beast, for it is the number of a man: His number is 666. (Revelation 13:16–18)

The number of man is 666 means the physical body. All people who put on a physical body and are born on this Earth take the mark of the beast (666). Jesus also took this mark because, without it, no one may buy or sell except one who has the mark or the name of the beast, or the number of his name. As the children are made of the flesh and the blood, He Himself became of the flesh and the blood means He took on a physical body.

Our soul is a currency (a denarius). As Jesus said to render to Caesar the things that are Caesar's, and to God the things that are God's. So, Jesus bought us by exchanging His life. The sin of debt that we had incurred, He paid off by giving up His life and freeing us.

"If thy brother be waxen poor, and hath sold away some of his possession, and if any of his kin come to redeem it, then shall he redeem that which his brother sold." (Leviticus 25:25 KJV)

This is how, when we were poor and pitiful, Jesus came and freed us. He is not ashamed to call us His brethren. We are related to Him.

Scriptures say, "Thus the heavens and the Earth were finished, and all the host of them. And on the seventh day God ended his work which he had made; and he rested on the seventh day from all his work which he had made" (Genesis 2:1–2 KJV). So, the seventh day represents completeness. The people who have destroyed the works of the flesh and killed the husband of sin, they will receive the mark of completeness which is 777. Those who have died to the flesh but are alive according to the Spirit.

"And I saw something like a sea of glass mingled with fire, and those who have the victory over the beast, over his image and over his mark and over the number of his name, standing on the sea of glass, having harps of God." (Revelation 15:2)

Jesus fought the war and was victorious over the beast, meaning the physical body (flesh) and He had the victory over his image and over his mark and over the number of his name. Those who accept Jesus as their Lord and follow Him are also victorious over the beast by the grace of our Lord Jesus Christ; they die out to the works of the devil. They die according to the flesh but are alive according to the Spirit.

Scripture says, "The God of peace will crush Satan under your feet shortly" (Romans 16:20). Thus, the devil (beast) means our physical body, which is only for 7,000 years, and, after that, all the visible things will go away and only the invisible will last.

Paul says, "And lest I should be exalted above measure by the abundance of the revelations, a thorn in the flesh was given to me, a messenger of Satan to buffet me, lest I be exalted above measure. Concerning this thing I pleaded with the Lord three times that it might depart from me. And He said to me, 'My grace is sufficient for you, for My strength is made perfect in weakness'" (2 Corinthians 12:7–9).

The thorn, which Paul is taking about, is the thorn that was given to him in the flesh, which was his physical body that lusts after worldly sin, which is a messenger of Satan. This is Paul's physical body for which Paul prays three times to God that this physical thorn in the flesh might be taken away from him that he can depart from this tent and be with the Lord. But, the Lord said to him, "My grace is sufficient for you." Because the race in this life was not completed for Paul. The plan of God for Paul and his life on this Earth was not completed yet that would bring God glory and the church edification.

63. Face of God

Scriptures say that no one has seen God at any time. The only begotten Son, who is in the bosom of the father, He has declared Him. That Son means Jesus and all those who are to be firstfruits with Jesus who have destroyed the works of the flesh and are alive according to the Spirit. "And Moses said, Thus saith the LORD, About midnight will I go out into the midst of Egypt: and all the firstborn in the land of Egypt shall die, from the firstborn of Pharaoh that sitteth upon his throne, even unto the firstborn of the maidservant that is behind the mill; and all the firstborn of beasts" (Exodus 11:4–5 KJV). Thus, God went into the midst of Egypt and the firstborn means the flesh that lusts after sin died seeing God. The firstborns of Israel were redeemed by the blood of the lamb. Jesus' blood covers our sins.

Firstborn means the first terrestrial body (flesh), then the spiritual body, so the flesh is the firstborn. During the time of Judges, when the Philistines took the ark of the covenant, God struck them with tumors and the plague. After that, they sent the ark of God on a new cart hitched with two cows. On the way, the men of Beth Shemesh looked into the ark of the Lord and the Lord struck them and they died because they saw God.

When David was bringing the ark of the covenant on an oxen cart, Uzza put out his hand to hold the ark for the oxen stumbled, and Uzza died. In the wilderness, when the people of Israel were dying because of the fiery serpent bites, Moses made a bronze serpent and put it on a pole. This serpent represents Jesus, whoever saw him and believed, they lived. The face of Jesus is the face of God. Jesus said, "He who has seen Me has seen the Father."

James says, "But he who looks into the perfect law of liberty and continues in it, and is not a forgetful hearer but a doer of the work, this one will be blessed in what he does" (James 1:25). The perfect law of liberty is Jesus, who was crucified for our sins, we see His face and continue to see it and obey His commandments. We die to the sinful works of the flesh and live according to the Spirit. Thus, Jesus' face is the face of God and no one can see God and live according to the flesh.

As Paul says, "The world has been crucified to me and I to the world."

Thus, we should continue to see the face of God and receive eternal inheritance, which is God.

64. Angel

"The angels who did not keep their proper domain, but left their own abode, He has reserved in everlasting chains under darkness for the judgment of the great day." (Jude 1:6)

Angels didn't keep their proper domain as the devil came to the woman and deceived the woman so that the woman saw the tree was good for food, that it was pleasant *to* the *eyes*, and a tree desirable *to* make one wise, she took of its fruit and ate. She also gave *to* her husband with her, and he ate. In the same way, the devil came to Jesus (second Adam) but Jesus didn't disobey and listen to the devil. *Serpent* represents a thought that encourages to fulfill the lust of the flesh. "For we do not have a High Priest who cannot sympathize with our weaknesses, but was in all points tempted as we are, yet without sin" (Hebrews 4:15). Thus, the Scriptures say, "Adam was not deceived, but the woman being deceived, fell into transgression" (1 Timothy 2:14). But Adam (Jesus) took the fruit from the woman and ate means He took our sins upon Himself and God punished the sin in His body on the cross and He suffered death.

Then the Lord God called to Adam and said to him, "Where are you?" So, he said, "I heard Your voice in the garden, and I was afraid because I was naked; and I hid myself" (Genesis 3:9–10).

Thus, Jesus suffered death. He took our sins and God left Him. Jesus said on the cross, "My God, My God, why have you forsaken Me?" Thus, Jesus was naked on the cross. For the joy that was set before Him, He endured the cross, despising the shame. He suffered death to receive us back and to give us life. As in hell, everyone is naked and without covering; Jesus became naked. Jesus said to the Father, "The glory which you have given me I have given them," means He gave us life and He took away death from us. He gave us His light and He took away darkness from us.

God called Adam and said, "Where are you?" because Adam had lost His domain. The way, angels did not keep their proper domain and left their abode, the first Adam disobeyed and left his domain and (one-third of the) angels that were in his loins (waist) also left their domain and sinned.

"Therefore, just as through one man sin entered the world, and death through sin, and thus death spread to all men, because all sinned" (Romans 5:12). "Although sin was already in the world before the law came but for where there is no law there is no transgression. Nevertheless, death reigned from Adam to Moses, even over those who had not sinned according to the likeness of the transgression of Adam, who is a type of Him who was to come" (Romans 5:13–14).

Thus, through one man, sin entered the world and sin brought death and we got separated from God and all fell into the darkness of hell. "For if God did not spare the angels who sinned but cast them down to hell and delivered them into chains of darkness, to be reserved for judgment" (2 Peter 2:4). Thus, they will be there until the last day. The eighth day means during the 8000s there will be the day of resurrection, to the resurrection of life, or to the resurrection of damnation.

But, we have freedom in Christ Jesus. Those who have not accepted Jesus Christ will be judged. Paul said, "Do not forget to entertain strangers, for by so doing some have unwittingly entertained angels." So, we are the one-third angels who left their abode.

> And it came to pass, when men began to multiply on the face of the Earth, and daughters were born unto them, that the sons of God saw the daughters of men that they were fair; and they took them wives of all which they chose. And the LORD said, My spirit shall not always strive with man, for that he also is flesh: yet his days shall be an hundred and twenty years. There were giants in the Earth in those days; and also after that, when the sons of God came in unto the daughters of men, and they bare children to them, the same became mighty men which were of old, men of renown.
>
> And GOD saw that the wickedness of man was great in the Earth, and that every imagination of the thoughts of his heart was only evil continually. And it repented the LORD that he had made man on the Earth, and it grieved him at his heart. And the LORD said, I will destroy man whom I have created from the face of the Earth; both man, and beast, and the creeping thing, and the fowls of the air; for it repenteth me that I have made them. But Noah found grace in the eyes of the LORD. (Genesis 6:1–8 KJV)

Daughters of men represent the flesh (physical body) and sons of God, who represent the spiritual body, took wives for themselves; of all whom they chose means they become one with the lust of the flesh. They became one with the flesh. God is a Spirit and, instead of (marrying) being one with Him, they become one with the lust of the flesh. In those days, there were giants on the Earth and sons of God came into the daughters of men and bore them mighty men of renown.

As James writes, "Each one is tempted when he is drawn away by his own desires and enticed. Then, when desire has conceived, it gives birth to sin; and sin, when it is fully grown, bring forth death" (James 1:14–15). Thus, we give birth to sin. In the days of Noah, they bore children to them. They were mighty men of renown. As there were in the beginning of the church, a man had his father's wife and committed sexual immorality. And they were puffed up rather than mourning about this matter. Thus, when sin was conceived, the mighty men of renown were born. The mighty men of renown represent our sins. The way Goliath challenged the Israelites for 40 days to war means our sins challenged God for 4,000 years.

Noah was a just man, perfect in his generations. Noah walked with God. Noah represents Jesus. He built an ark of faith and seven in that ark were saved when they were disobedient. The blood of Jesus cleanses us from all sins and by faith in Him, we are saved.

Noah and his family went into the ark, and seven pairs of clean animals and two pairs of unclean animals were taken with them. And it rained for forty days and forty nights. These forty days and nights represent 4,000 years in which the Israelites were in bondage in Egypt; they were in the bondage of sin. Thus, it rained forty days and nights, and on that day, all the fountains of the great deep were broken up, this represents the daughters of man (physical body), and the windows of heaven were opened and rained, these represent the sons of God (spiritual body) who were rulers of the heaven became one with the daughters of man and sinned. By them, mighty men of renown (sins) were born. Thus, the (one-third) angels didn't keep their proper domain and left their abode and reaped destruction for themselves.

"And another sign appeared in heaven: behold, a great, fiery red dragon having seven heads and ten horns, and seven diadems on his heads. His tail drew a third of the stars of heaven and threw them to the Earth" (Revelation 12:3–4). This tail represents the lust of the flesh by which a third of the stars (sons of God) fell on Earth. That tail (lust of the flesh) became ruler over them (sons of God). But God said, you will be the head and not the tail. God has sent us here to rule on the Earth, but we became slaves of the lust of the flesh. We are the heads, as the Scriptures say, "You are gods, and all of you are children of the Most High" (Psalm 82.6).

"And the stars of heaven fell to the Earth, as a fig tree drops its late figs when it is shaken by a mighty wind" (Revelation 12:3). As a fig tree drops its late figs, the stars of heaven fell to the Earth, and we fell into the darkness. We should not be late figs but be mature and fight against the darkness.

When the Israelites entered into the Promised Land, God left the lords of the Philistines, all the Canaanites, the Sidonians, and the Hivites in the land so that the generations of the children of Israel might be taught to know war who had not formerly known war. The way Jesus fought with the darkness and being victorious, sat on the throne with God, we should also become perfect as our Father in heaven is perfect under the grace of Jesus Christ.

In the days of Noah, there were the mighty men of renown, meaning the sins, they were rebellious against God and God made them visible. Goliath is an example of that. He was rebellious against God, and he (sins) challenged God for forty days, meaning 4,000 years. He stood and cried out to the armies of Israel, and said to them to choose a man for themselves, and let him come down to fight and, if he is able to kill him, then they will be their servants. But if Goliath prevails against him and kills him, then the Israelites will be their servants and will serve the Philistines. And the Philistine said, "I defy the armies of Israel this day, give me a man, that we may fight together." And God chose David who represents Jesus and David said, "Who is this uncircumcised Philistine, that he should defy the armies of the living God?" Then Saul said to David, "You are not able to go against this Philistine to fight with him; for you are a youth." But David replied, "Your servant used to keep his father's sheep, and when a lion or a bear came and took a lamb out of the flock, I went out after it and struck it, and delivered the lamb from its mouth; and when it arose against me, I caught it by its beard, and struck and killed it. The Lord, who delivered me from the paw of the lion and from the paw of the bear, He will deliver me from the hand of this Philistine."

David represents Jesus, he put his hand in his bag and took out a stone; and he slung it and struck the Philistine in his forehead, so that the stone sank into his forehead, and he fell on his face to the Earth. So, David prevailed over the Philistine with a sling and a stone (the law) and struck the Philistine and killed him. Thus, David killed Goliath with a stone, meaning by the law, and destroyed our sins. In the same way, Jesus took our sins upon Himself and died on the cross and destroyed sin. Jesus by obedience fulfilled and established the law. Thus, Jesus killed Goliath who rebelled against God.

Paul writes, "For indeed He does not give aid to angels, but He does give aid to the seed of Abraham" (Hebrews 2:16). This means whoever believed in Jesus are the seed of Abraham and God gives aid to them. The angels who do not believe in Jesus will perish. Jesus said, "Most assuredly, I say to you, hereafter you shall see heaven open, and the angels of God ascending and descending upon the Son of Man" (John 1:51). Jesus has become a mediator for those who believe in Him, and they can reach God. The way is open for them.

According to the Letter to Hebrews, in these last days, God spoke to us by His Son whom He has appointed heir of all things, through whom also He made the worlds. He is being the brightness of His glory and the express image of His person. For to which of the angels did He ever say that You are My Son, Today I have begotten You? Thus, Jesus who is an angel, God said this for Him.

When He again brings the firstborn into the world, He says: "Let all the angels of God worship Him" (Hebrews 1:6) means we worship the Lord Jesus.

"You have loved righteousness and hated lawlessness; Therefore God, Your God, has anointed You With the oil of gladness more than Your companions." (Hebrews 1:9)

To which of the angles did He ever say as, "The Lord said to my Lord, 'Sit at My right hand, Till I make Your enemies Your footstool'" (Psalm 110:1). David said, "The Lord said to my Lord (Jesus), sit at my right hand till I make Your enemies Your footstool." Jesus is seated at the right hand of God and on the eighth day He will be resurrected, and Jesus in His glory will sit on the throne. New heaven and new Earth, Jesus (son of David) will reign forever. Amen.

65. Lucifer

The name *Lucifer* means "morning star" (sun) and "light bearer," that which brings light. *Lucifer* means Jesus' physical body, who took all of our sins upon Himself. Thus, the sun became black.

We made our physical body our God and obeyed all its commandments and fulfilled all the lusts of the flesh. The physical body that was created from the dirt, we worshipped that idol and made it our God.

> Son of man, take up a lamentation for the king of Tyre, and say to him, "Thus says the Lord God: 'You were the seal of perfection, Full of wisdom and perfect in beauty. You were in Eden, the garden of God; Every precious stone was your covering: The sardius, topaz, and diamond, Beryl, onyx, and jasper, Sapphire, turquoise, and emerald with gold. The work-

manship of your timbrels and pipes was prepared for you on the day you were created. You were the anointed cherub who covers; I established you; You were on the holy mountain of God; You walked back and forth in the midst of fiery stones. You were perfect in your ways from the day you were created, till iniquity was found in you.'" (Ezekiel 28:12–15)

Thus, God created Lucifer in the Garden of Eden. Jesus was the beginning of the creation of God. Lucifer, Jesus and Adam these three are the same person. It's written that You were perfect in your ways from the day you were created till iniquity was found in you means Jesus was perfect until He took our sins upon Himself. He was perfect until He took the forbidden fruit from the woman and ate.

This is how Jesus joined together with the woman, became one with her and committed adultery, and gave us His glory and took our darkness. Thus, the sun became black.

"By the abundance of your trading You became filled with violence within, and you sinned; Therefore I cast you as a profane thing Out of the mountain of God; And I destroyed you, O covering cherub, From the midst of the fiery stones" (Ezekiel 28:16).

By the abundance of your trading, you became filled with violence within, and you sinned. The sins we committed are as currencies of this world and we do trade with them. Jesus took those sins upon Himself and through worldly trading became rich. Thus, God cast Him out as a profane thing out of the mountain of God. Thus, Jesus sacrificed His physical body on the cross and God cast Him out from the place of God.

> And war broke out in heaven: Michael and his angels fought with the dragon; and the dragon and his angels fought, but they did not prevail, nor was a place found for them in heaven any longer. So, the great dragon was cast out, that serpent of old, called the Devil and Satan, who deceives the whole world; he was cast to the Earth, and his angels were cast out with

him. Then I heard a loud voice saying in heaven, "Now salvation, and strength, and the kingdom of our God, and the power of His Christ have come, for the accuser of our brethren, who accused them before our God Day and night, has been cast down." (Revelation 12:7–10)

The Scripture says, "Then the seventy returned with joy, saying, 'Lord, even the demons are subject to us in Your name.' And He (Jesus) said to them, 'I saw Satan fall like lightning from heaven'" (Luke 10:17–18).

Now, God didn't give place to Satan in heaven. *Michael* means gift of God who represents Jesus, Him, and all the angels who followed Him fought with the dragon and His angels who represents the physical body. Jesus and His angels who are the spiritual body, who walk according to the Spirit, fought the war and defeated Satan. Thus, Jesus crushed the devil's head.

"You defiled your sanctuaries, By the multitude of your iniquities, By the iniquity of your trading; Therefore, I brought fire from your midst; It devoured you, And I turned you to ashes upon the Earth in the sight of all who saw you" (Ezekiel 28:18).

Abimelech, the son of Jerubbaal, wanted to be a king over Israel who represents Jesus. He killed his brothers, the seventy sons of Jerubbaal, on one stone means by the stone that represents the law, through that law he killed them according to the sinful works of the flesh. Likewise, Abimelech was also killed by a woman who dropped an upper millstone on Abimelech's head and crushed his skull. Thus, God killed Abimelech by a woman. Thus, God gave glory to the woman to destroy the devil. Deborah said to Barak that God will give glory to woman to kill Sisera.

When Abimelech killed his brothers, the seventy sons of Jerubbaal, on one stone. But Jotham, the youngest son of Jerubbaal, was left because he hid himself. He said to the people of Shechem, "You have made Abimelech, the son of a female servant, king over the men of Shechem." This means the (bond) servant who is a slave of sin. He says of that, "If then you have acted in truth and sincerity with Jerubbaal and with his house this day, then rejoice in Abimelech, and let him also rejoice in you. But if not, let fire come from Abimelech and devour the men of Shechem and Beth Millo; and let fire come from the men of Shechem and from Beth Millo and devour Abimelech!" (Judges 9:19–20). Thus, fire came from Abimelech, and he was devoured by the fire, meaning sin was destroyed. The physical body is sowed, and the spiritual is raised.

> How you are fallen from heaven, O Lucifer, son of the morning! How you are cut down to the ground, You who weakened the nations! For you have said in your heart: "I will ascend into heaven, I will exalt my throne above the stars of God; I will also sit on the mount of the congregation on the farthest sides of the north; I will ascend above the heights of the clouds, I will be like the Most High." Yet you shall be brought down to Sheol, To the lowest depths of the Pit. "Those who see you will gaze at you, and consider you, saying: 'Is this the man who made the Earth tremble, Who shook kingdoms, Who made the world as a wilderness And destroyed its cities, Who did not open the house of his prisoners?'" (Isaiah 14:12–16)

I will ascend above the heights of the clouds, I will be like the Most High. Yet you shall be brought down to Sheol. Jesus took our sins upon Himself and destroyed them, removed them as far as east is from the west. He removed them so far that He went to the lowest depths of the Pit.

Those who see you will gaze at you, and consider you, saying, "Is this the man who made this Earth tremble, who shook kingdoms, who made the world as a wilderness and destroyed its cities, who did not open the house of his prisoners?"

That Satan is your physical body which lusts after sin and makes you a prisoner. But whoever believes in the name of Jesus and follows Him carrying the cross, crucifies the sinful flesh and dies to the works of the flesh; they all live according to the Spirit and live to God. Blessed is that man!

For you have said in your heart that I will ascend into heaven, I will exalt my throne above the stars of God. I will also sit on the mount of the congregation on the farthest sides of the north; I will ascend above the heights of the clouds, I will be like the Most High.

Lucifer wanted to exalt his throne above the stars of God. The stars of God represent brethren. He wanted to exalt his status above all his brethren, and I will be like the Most High, meaning I will be equal to God.

During the time of the Tower of Babel, the whole Earth had one language. And they said, "Come, let us build ourselves a city, and a tower whose top is in the heavens; let us make a name for ourselves, lest we be scattered abroad over the face of the whole Earth" (Genesis 11:4).

The Tower of Babel represents the physical body; let us build a tower whose top is in the heaven. Heaven is His throne. Thus, people wanted to be equal to God through their physical body. But God came down and changed their languages. Therefore, God gave another tongue, gave us the Holy Spirit, so that not by the physical body but by the Spirit we can be equal to God. "Therefore, you shall be perfect, just as your Father in heaven is perfect" (Matthew 5:48).

Thus, Jesus was raised from the dead through the Spirit and was exalted above all His brethren and God made Him Christ and the Lord. Jesus is seated at the right hand of God and became equal to God. Thus, God says, "Through the Spirit, become equal to God."

"Therefore, God also has highly exalted Him and given Him the name which is above every name." (Philippians 2:9)

66. Victory

Jesus fought with the darkness and won. He was in all points tempted as we are, yet without sin.

"He shall rule them (Gentiles) with a rod of iron; They shall be dashed to pieces like the potter's vessels—as I also have received from My Father." (Revelation 2:27)

Jesus was victorious over darkness, and He said to us, "In the world you will have tribulation, but be of good cheer, I have overcome the world." Jesus leads us with triumph. Thus, Jesus won, and God gave Him the revelation about the future and Jesus gave that to John so that John can make that known to the church. John wrote the Book of Revelation of Jesus that is the last book in the Bible.

"He who has an ear, let him hear what the Spirit says to the churches. To him who overcomes I will give to eat from the tree of life, which is in the midst of the Paradise of God." (Revelation 2:7)

He who overcomes, will not have to suffer the second death. "To whom he overcomes I will give some of the hidden manna to eat. And I will give him a white stone, and on the stone a new name written which no one knows except him who receives it." (Revelation 2:17)

"And he who overcomes, and keeps My works until the end, to him I will give power over the nations." (Revelation 2:26)

"He who overcomes, I will make him a pillar in the temple of My God, and he shall go out no more. I will write on him the name of My God and the name of the city of My God, the New Jerusalem, which comes down out of heaven from My God. And I will write on him My new name." (Revelation 3:12)

"To him who overcomes I will grant to sit with Me on My throne, as I also overcame and sat down with My Father on His throne" (Revelation 3:21) means He became equal to God. Thus, you also become perfect as God your Father is. It is enough that a servant becomes like his master. Be faithful until death, and Jesus will give you the crown of life.

"His (Jesus') eyes were like a flame of fire, and on His head were many crowns. He had a name written that no one knew except Himself." (Revelation 19:12)

I also had a vision of crown. A gold crown was placed on my head, then a white diamond crown was placed on my head, and then a third crown with red diamonds was placed on my head. The crowns were given to me one after the other. But Jesus' head had many crowns that could not be numbered.

I had a dream one night where I was lying down under a glorious black mulberry tree. That tree was tall and spread out. That tree had lots of ripened black mulberries in a bunch. Each bunch had five to six mulberries and the branches of the tree were very low that I was able to pick mulberries while lying down under the tree. While eating, I got up and one bunch of mulberries fell that I caught in my hand. I felt as though that tree was in heaven.

When I was writing this book, God the Father talked to me saying that, "What I asked, you have written every word not leaving a single word." Then He reminded me of this dream that I didn't let the bunch of mulberries fall on the ground.

Bible Scriptures are also like mulberries in a bunch. When we understand all Scriptures from the whole Bible, only then we can truly understand. The way the pillars of the temple were decorated with a network of bronze pomegranates all the way around, the Bible is the same way. Jesus said, "To him who overcomes I will give to eat from the tree of life."

About five years ago, during communion in our church, our pastor Ketan Gurjar was leading prayer and worship. I was worshiping with my eyes closed and a drop of the blood of Jesus fell on my head, I felt that in my spirit. After church, I shared that with my sister. After that, I forgot about it and, in these days, God reminded me and said, "You have a part in the first resurrection, you have a part in the 144,000, the way Lazarus was raised on the fourth day, you have a part in the first resurrection with Jesus." He has redeemed many souls by His blood. Amen.

67. Pool of Siloam

> Now as Jesus passed by, He saw a man who was blind from birth. And His disciples asked Him, saying, "Rabbi, who sinned, this man or his parents, that he was born blind?" Jesus answered, "Neither this man nor his parents sinned, but that the works of God should be revealed in him. I must work the works of Him who sent Me while it is day; the night is coming when no one can work. As long as I am in the world, I am the light of the world." When He had said these things, He spat on the ground and made clay with the saliva; and He anointed the eyes of the blind the clay. And He said to him, "Go, wash in the pool of Siloam" (which is translated, Sent). So he went and washed, and came back seeing. (John 9:1–7)

The blind man from birth represents the people of Earth. God sent us blind in this world, but we were already taught by God. We experienced darkness for 4,000 years, were slave to darkness. Jesus came during the 4000s and opened our eyes so that we can see the light and see how God is.

Jesus said, "Neither this man nor his parents sinned, but that the works of God should be revealed in him." We see God and follow Him, and His works are revealed in us. His love is revealed.

The way the father gave the portion of inheritance to the prodigal son and sent him to experience. The time on this Earth has been given to us as a resource to educate. When the prodigal son came to himself, he said that the father is good.

If we have experienced darkness, then we will be able to recognize that the light is good. If we suffer the sun's heat, we will appreciate the shade. Our works of the darkness establishes God's light. Our unrighteousness demonstrates the righteousness of God.

Jesus said, "For judgment I have come into this world, that those who do not see may see, and that those who see may be made blind" (John 9:39).

The people of Israel have God's words and they could see. Paul said, "For I do not desire, brethren, that you should be ignorant of this mystery" (Romans 11:25). We were blind before and experienced the darkness. Now the people of Israel were made blind so they can experience the darkness. "For as you were once disobedient to God, yet have now obtained mercy through their disobedience, even so these also have now been disobedient, that through the mercy shown you they also may obtain mercy. For God has committed them all to disobedience, that He might have mercy on all" (Romans 11:30–32).

When I was twenty-one years old, I got saved and accepted Jesus; before that, I was blind toward God and could not see God. When Jesus came into my life as the light, I saw the works of darkness within me, and I repented of those sins.

EIGHT

LIFE ON EARTH

68. Sin

"If anyone sees his brother sinning a sin which does not lead to death, he will ask, and He will give him life for those who commit sin not leading to death. There is sin leading to death. I do not say that he should pray about that. All unrighteousness is sin, and there is sin not leading to death." (1 John 5:16–17)

Jesus said, "Anyone who speaks a word against the Son of Man, it will be forgiven him; but whoever speaks against the Holy Spirit, it will not be forgiven him, either in this age or in the age to come" (Matthew 12:32).

"Therefore, if you bring your gift to the altar, and there remember that your brother has something against you, leave your gift there before the altar, and go your way. First be reconciled to your brother, and then come and offer your gift." (Matthew 5:23–24)

If we do not reconcile with our brother, our sacrifice, our gift on the altar, is not acceptable to God. The way five foolish virgins didn't take oil with them and their lamps went out. They stopped doing the good works, and the fire of the Holy Spirit went out. Scripture says, "Do not quench the Spirit, but they quenched the Spirit." Thus, they were not accepted to enter the life, but were separated from God forever.

They blasphemed against the Holy Spirit, and they refused to accept God's word and to do God's works. That is the sin leading to death, with that we suffer second death.

Jesus said, anyone who speaks a word against the Son of Man, it will be forgiven him. The Son of Man means the physical body, which lusts after the flesh and sins against God. If we curse the works of the flesh, the evil works of the flesh will die out. If anyone sees his brother sinning that sin, he should ask God and He will give him life.

When Jesus cursed the fig tree, that fig tree represented Jesus' soul. Jesus took our sins upon Himself and brought death to sin, and God gave Him life from the dead.

69. Image of God

Then God said, "Let Us make man in Our image, according to Our likeness and let them have dominion over the all the Earth." So, God created man in His own image, He created him, male and female. Then God blessed them, and God said to them, "Be be fruitful and multiply and fill the Earth and subdue it, have dominion over all the Earth."

"This is the book of the generations of Adam. In the day that God created man, in the likeness of God made he him; male and female created he them; and blessed them, and called their name Adam, in the day when they were created" (Genesis 5:1–2 KJV). The meaning of *Adam* is Earth.

God took one of Adam's ribs and closed up the flesh in its place and made into a woman, And Adam said: "This is now bone of my bones, and flesh of my flesh; She shall be called Woman. Because she was taken out of Man." Therefore, a man shall leave his father and mother and be joined to his wife, and they shall become one flesh.

After Jesus was resurrected from the dead, He came to His disciples and said, See, for a spirit does not have flesh and bones as you see I have." The way Adam said, "The bone of my bone and flesh of my flesh, you shall be called Woman."

"For by Him all things were created that are in heaven and that are on Earth, visible and invisible, whether thrones or dominions or principalities or powers. All things were created through Him and for Him" (Colossian 1:16). This is the Gospel of His Son and everything was created through Him and for Him and His name is Jesus Christ.

Thus, Jesus created woman out of Himself that is His woman and Paul said, "I may present you (the woman) as a chaste virgin to Christ who is winkle free and without blemish." So, we are Christ's helper.

God created Adam first and then woman.

"And to the angel of the church of the Laodiceans write, 'These things says the Amen, the Faithful and True Witness, the Beginning of the creation of God'" (Revelation 3:14). God created Adam and God lived inside of Adam. Adam (Jesus) wanted to eat the fruit of the tree of the knowledge of good and evil. But, as three men comes to meet Abraham, God is a man and, in the same way, Jesus was a man (spiritual) and was very strong. As Scriptures say, "God who cannot lie and God who cannot ever sin, in the same way, Adam could never eat the fruit of the tree of the knowledge of good and evil. Whatever was invisible, that became visible."

"Man (Adam) is the image and glory of God; but woman is the glory of man." (1 Corinthians 11:7)

Thus, God created a helper for Adam, woman who is a weaker vessel; therefore, woman took the fruit of the tree of the knowledge of good and evil and ate and was subjected to the devil. Earth was also subjected to futility because of Him who subjected it. If we have our physical body only, then we can sin and experience darkness; without it, we cannot sin.

Luke 15:11–22—Prodigal Son Parable Explanation

A certain man has two sons. The elder son, which is Jesus, and the younger son means us. And the younger son asked his father to give his portion of goods that falls to him and went to a far country. He went away from the father and wasted all his possessions with prodigal living. Ecclesiastes says, "There is time and season for everything and God-given task with which the sons of men are to be occupied on this Earth," so that being away from the father, we can learn and experience everything on this Earth. After that, when we come to ourselves and realize like the prodigal son and we go back to the father and say, "Father, I have sinned against heaven, and in thy sight, and am no more worthy to be called thy son, make me as one of thy hired servants." The way when one sinner repents and there is joy in heaven, the Father says, "Bring forth the best robe, and put it on him; and put a ring on his hand, and shoes on his feet: and bring hither the fatted calf, and kill it; and let us eat, and be merry: for this my son was dead to me and was dead to my works but is alive again; he was lost, and is found."

As Jesus said, "For the Son of man is come to seek and to save that which was lost." Peter said, "For we have spent enough of our past lifetime in doing the useless things, now live for the will of God." Therefore, you shall be perfect, just as your Father in heaven is, and have the same nature as He has. But the elder son was angry, and would not go in: Therefore, his father came out and pleaded with him and said, "Son, you are always with me, and all that I have is yours." But it pleased the Lord to bruise Him. Thus, Jesus scarified Himself to save us. Jesus took all of our sins upon Himself, Adam (Jesus) took the fruit of the tree of knowledge of good and evil from the woman (us) and ate and experienced sin. Jesus did not commit any sin, but He took our sins upon Himself and gave us His glory which God had given Him. And Jesus said to His disciples, "You are the light of the world."

"Nevertheless, neither is man independent of woman, nor woman independent of man, in the Lord. For as woman came from man, even so man also comes through woman; but all things are from God." (1 Corinthians 11:11–12)

So, Jesus (Adam) took the fruit of the tree of the knowledge of good and evil from the woman and ate and, by doing this, He went to the depths of darkness. The way God is omnipresent, Jesus also became omnipresent. As David says, "If I ascend into heaven, You are there; If I make my bed in hell, behold, You are there." So, God is everywhere. "Even though I walk through the valley of the shadow of death, I will fear no evil; For You are with me." Thus, Jesus stepped down into the darkness, fought against the darkness, defeated it, and become mature and omnipresent.

"His (Jesus') head and hair were white like wool, as white as snow, and His eyes like a flame of fire" (Revelation 1:14). *White hair* represents maturity. Jesus has won every battle and is victorious over every nation.

"And the stars of heaven fell to the Earth, as a fig tree drops its late figs when it is shaken by a mighty wind" (Revelation 6:13). The way the fig tree drops its late figs because of the wind, the stars of heaven (one-third angels), which are late figs, fell to the Earth to become mature. Thus, Man that is Jesus who experienced darkness by taking the fruit from the woman and the woman experienced the light and the glory through Jesus. Man is not independent of woman or woman independent of man. If they are together, only then they are called *God*. Thus, God's image is man and woman together, God's image is male and female. If they are separated from each other, they are not God.

"For this reason, a man shall leave his father and mother and be joined to his wife, and the two shall become one flesh. This is a great mystery, but I speak concerning Christ and the church" (Ephesians 5:31–32). Christ is the one who defeated death and was raised from the dead, and the church is the one who gives their burden of sin to Jesus Christ and takes His light yoke and becomes one with Him.

"Let no one say when he is tempted, 'I am tempted by God'; for God cannot be tempted by evil, nor does He Himself tempt anyone. But each one is tempted when he is drawn away by his own desires and enticed. Then, when desire has conceived, it gives birth to sin; and sin, when it is full-grown, brings forth death" (James 1:13–15). Thus, we ourselves are drawn to sin. He, who deceives others, deceives himself and, whoever sets up a trap for others, gets caught himself. So, whatever happens and the sins we commit, we are responsible for them. We should repent from our sins and go back to the Father.

70. God's Image Is Man and Woman

"He is the image of the invisible God, the firstborn over all creation." (1 Colossians 1:15)

"(The Son) who being the brightness of His glory and the express image of His person." (Hebrews 1:3)

Thus, Jesus is exactly the same as God the Father, who is the invisible God that we can see now in Jesus Christ.

There is man and woman both in Jesus. Woman that is physical body and man that is spiritual body. If we walk according to the flesh, we are physical, carnal; but, if we walk according to the Spirit, we are sons of God and are spiritual. So, our soul should be underfoot, the physical body should be under our authority. Therefore, God said that you are head and not tail. So, we should not make our soul our head but, instead, do the same as God, the heaven is His tabernacle, and the Earth is His footstool, meaning Earth representing God's soul, He keeps the soul underfoot.

When I had a vision of God, the Earth was under His feet. Thus, God has called us to be rulers in our lives. As many as walk according to the Spirit, He gives them the right to be the sons of God.

God the Father made a new covenant to make our flesh the footstool in our lives. Do not walk according to the flesh. For to be carnally minded is death, but to be spiritually minded is life and peace. So, the old carnally minded lifestyle be destroyed, and we should become spiritual. This is why Jesus obeyed all commandments, obeyed all the law, and died on the cross, and calling it old covenant made that obsolete. Now, what is becoming obsolete and growing old is ready to vanish away. After 7,000 years, there will be a new heaven and new Earth.

Thus, Jesus is the express image of the invisible God. He is God's only Son, but with Him, we received the right to be adopted sons by whom we cry out, "Abba, Father."

God created man in His own image. Jesus is the beginning of God's creation. He was created by God. After suffering death on the cross, God raised Him from the dead on the third day. He was declared to be the Son of God with the power according to the Spirit of holiness, by the resurrection from the dead.

God's image is man and woman both. If they are together, only then they are called *God* and, if they are separated, they are not God. Neither is man independent of woman nor woman independent of man; in the Lord, if they are together, then they are God.

All that is invisible; God has made visible and revealed them to us.

"Nevertheless, she will be saved in childbearing (divine Son) if they continue in faith, love, and holiness, with self-control" (1 Timothy 2:15). So, we should be saved by giving birth to a son.

Thus, we should decide if we, as man, meaning walking according to the Spirit, want to give birth to a son or, as woman, meaning walking according to the flesh, be destroyed.

Therefore, God the Father has kept His Seed in us, so that we can give birth to a son. If He had not kept His Seed, we would have been destroyed a long time ago.

When man ate the fruit of the knowledge of good and evil, God the Father drove out the man and He placed a cherubim at the east of the Garden of Eden and a flaming sword, which turned every way, to guard the way to the tree of life, lest he put out his hand and take also of the tree of life, and eat, and live forever. So that seed of the tree of life was kept aside and, once the time was fulfilled, that Seed was revealed when Jesus Christ came on this Earth. He was seen by angels. Every angel saw Him and they, who were separated from God the Father, are reconciled to God through Jesus Christ.

The tree of life represents the spiritual body and the tree of the knowledge of good and evil represents the physical body. *Eden* means in the Earth God created, the garden, and in the midst of the garden a tree of life and a tree of the knowledge of good and evil.

These two trees are both God's seed. We are not one, but we are two. Abraham represents God the Father and He has two sons. The way Abraham had two sons. Ishmael represents the physical body, which is the tree of the knowledge of good and evil. It has more than one personality which hides its own evil by pretending to be good. There is no one good but God. Isaac represents the spiritual body, which represents the tree of life. Paul said, "However, the spiritual is not first, but the natural, and afterward the spiritual (1 Corinthians 15:46). And God said about Ishmael, "He too is the seed of Abraham, and I will make a nation of Ishmael." The time for the physical life is only for 7,000 years and, after that, physical life will go away and only the spiritual will last. God will convert our mortal bodies into glorified bodies.

The scripture said, "Shall I give my firstborn for my transgression, the fruit of my body for the sin of my soul?" (Micah 6:7 KJV)

So, God sacrifices the firstborn, meaning the physical body. "Now I saw a new heaven and a new Earth, for the first heaven and the first Earth had passed away. Also there was no more sea" (Revelation 21:1).

God said, "For the sin of my soul, shall I sacrifice the fruit of my body (the physical body)?" The one-third angels who did not keep their proper domain but left their own abode were part of God Himself. Those who did not keep their proper domain, but become one with the lusts of the flesh, were one-third angels who fell from God. They are a part of God, a part of His body. God is a double part (two-thirds), meaning He is double in strength and so He is the man and the one-third that fell were called woman because they were weaker; woman is a weaker vessel. Even so, there is neither male nor female, for you are all one in Christ Jesus because, in the kingdom of God, we will be like angels.

We were inside of God from the beginning, that's why we were already taught by God. Therefore, He chose us in Christ Jesus before the foundation of the world, that we should be holy and without blame before Him in love. The spirit God has given us He wants to receive back to Himself with joy.

Jesus said that He came forth from the Father in the same way we were inside of the Father before and we were sent on this Earth and, defeating the physical body by the Spirit, we are to go back to the Father. "He who overcomes I will grant to sit with Me on My throne," meaning we need to overcome and become like the Father. Jesus said, "I go back to the Father, and He went up to the Father in front of over 500 people and became equal to God and sat down at the right hand of the throne of God."

Samson said, "I will take revenge on the Philistines for my two eyes!" This physical body had made us blind relative to God. The Dagon god's temple where Samson was represents the physical body. The temple we have made a den of thieves. Samson destroyed that temple. Thus, God through Jesus Christ fought the war for us and took vengeance. Samson said, "Let me die but I will take vengeance." Then, the physical body was put to death.

The way Jesus was crucified and died and on the third day was raised from the dead through the power of the Holy Spirit, we should walk in His steps as He has given us example. So that we present our bodies a living sacrifice, holy, acceptable to God, and Jesus, who is the chief cornerstone with Him, being fitted together grow into a holy temple.

It was in the heart of David to build a temple for the name of the Lord God, but God said, "You shall not build the temple, but your son (Solomon) shall build the temple for My name." David, according to the old covenant, represents the physical body and Solomon the spiritual body. And God said that you have shed much blood so you should not build the temple but your son, meaning Jesus will build that temple. David also represents God the Father.

The way we give birth to a son, God the Father also gives birth to a Son. God the Father is a man and the Earth (His soul) represents woman. God the Father sends His Holy Spirit on the Earth so that the Holy Spirit would overshadow the people of the Earth, meaning He gives them the commandments and seed (Jesus) so they die to the works of the flesh and give birth to a son. And God said, "You are my Son, today I have begotten you." That Son is Jesus and those who will be firstfruits with Him. The son of David will reign forever. He is the son of God whom God has given birth to.

The kingdom became God's and of Jesus Christ and we are to be one with God.

"(He was) without father, without mother, without genealogy, having neither beginning of days nor end of life, but made like the Son of God, remains a priest continually" (Hebrews 7:3). This is Jesus Christ.

The way Jesus came from the Father, we were also sent to this Earth. Jesus said to us to follow Him, He obeyed all commandments and died related to sin. But God raised Him from the dead, so that He can live to God and go back to God the Father. We too need to go back to the Father and to do this as Jesus has given us the example. As Jesus did, we should die out to the works of the flesh, be resurrected by the Spirit, and become firstfruits with Jesus. He is seated at the right hand of the throne of God the Father. He has become equal to God.

The Son who is sitting in the bosom of the Father, of whom God said that, "You are my Son and today I have begotten you," Jesus and those who will be firstfruits with Him are those who have seen the Father and, besides them, no one has seen the Father.

Jesus said, "I am the beginning and the end." We were a part of God from the beginning but, because of the sin, we were separated from God. But now, we need to go back to the Father.

Paul said, "Do you not know that those who run in a race all run, but one receives the prize? Run in such a way that you may obtain it" (1 Corinthians 9:24).

The bride that will marry Jesus Christ is those who are to be firstfruits with Jesus, and they have a part in the first resurrection. Those who are alive and have not killed the husband of sin are those who are under the law and they are guests in the wedding feast. But, those who have not accepted God are Gentiles and they are dead related to God. They will be cast out and the door will be shut for them for eternity.

If God the Father had not kept the Seed for us, we would have perished a long time ago. The woman's seed is Jesus Christ who God kept hidden. Now, the great mystery of God that was hidden for ages was revealed in this age. "Many prophets and righteous men desired to see what you see, and did not see it, and to hear what you hear, and did not hear it" (Matthew 13:17). Jesus was born on this Earth and was seen by angels (1 Timothy 3:16).

Reuben the firstborn of Israel went up to his father's bed and committed fornication with his father's concubine. Reuben represents Jesus who committed fornication with his father's woman. *Woman* means all of the mankind, who Jesus become one with on the cross and took away our darkness, giving us His glory that God had given Him. Thus, God's seed was revealed to us.

During the time of Elijah, the heavens were shut for three-and-half years, meaning for 3,500 years it did not rain. The people of the Old Testament had not received grace; they were obeying the law through the flesh. They lived by obeying the commandments. If they broke the commandments, God's wrath came upon them.

"These are the generations of the heavens and of the Earth when they were created, in the day that the LORD God made the Earth and the heavens, and every plant of the field before it was in the Earth, and every herb of the field before it grew: for the LORD God had not caused it to rain upon the Earth . . . ."(Genesis 2:4–5 KJV)

Rain represents grace. "For the law was given through Moses, but grace and truth came through Jesus Christ" (John 1:17). Thus, after 3,500 years, it rained when the Seed was revealed to us. And, whoever has been born of God does not sin, for His seed remains in him. Thus, God has planted us on this Earth so that by Jesus' grace we can grow and bear fruits for God.

Joseph (Jesus), whose star was above the stars of his brothers, his brothers' stars bow down to his star. So, God has exalted Jesus over all His brothers and made Him Christ and the Lord. But, Jesus is not ashamed to call us His brethren. We increase in faith and love by the grace of Jesus and bring forth fruits for God the Father, some thirtyfold, some sixty, and some a hundred.

These are the generations of the heavens and of the Earth when they were created, in the day that the LORD God made the Earth and the heavens, and every plant of the field before it was in the Earth, and every herb of the field before it grew: for the LORD God had not caused it to rain upon the Earth, and there was not a man to till the ground. But there went up a mist from the Earth, and watered the whole face of the ground. And the LORD God formed man of the dust of the ground, and breathed into his nostrils the breath of life; and man became a living soul. (Genesis 2:4–7 KJV)

This is the history of the heavens and of the Earth when they were created. God had not caused it to rain and no herb of the field had grown on Earth. But a mist went up from the Earth and watered the whole face of the ground and God formed a man (Jesus) of the dust of the ground. And God breathed into His nostrils the breath of life. "And when He (Jesus) had said this, He breathed on them, and said to them, 'Receive the Holy Spirit'" (John 20:22). "In Him was life, and the life was the light of men" (John 1:4). And man became a living being.

Jesus is the beginning of God's creation (Revelation 3:14). Jesus was created first. God created man on the sixth day. Man was made perfect on the sixth day, and Jesus said on the cross that it is finished. Adam that is Son of God. "(God) has in these last days spoken to us by His Son, whom He has appointed heir of all things, through whom also He made the worlds" (Hebrews 1:2).

Adam and Eve were naked, but were not ashamed, the way babies are born on this Earth naked. This is how Jesus was born on this Earth, He came as zero. And He suffered and learned obedience. He obeyed all commandments perfectly and fully received God.

Jesus is the express image of God. When He was crucified, He took our darkness by taking our sins upon Himself and gave us His glory that God had given Him. He was naked on the cross,

His clothes, meaning the righteousness that He clothes us with. Thus, He covered our nakedness. Job (Jesus) said, "Naked came I out of my mother's womb, and naked shall I return thither: the LORD gave, and the LORD hath taken away; blessed be the name of the LORD" (Job 1:21 KJV).

He suffered death on the cross and gave us life and, by doing this, He redeemed us by His blood. The way the prodigal son returns to the Father, and the Father clothes him with the best robe, puts ring on his hand, and says that for this my son was dead related to God and is alive again; he was lost and is found. And God the Father rejoices.

Thus, grace (rain) came through Jesus. Jesus said on the cross, "It is finished," and He made man perfect. Jesus is our perfection.

71. Sacrifice

"And Solomon loved the LORD, walking in the statutes of David his father: only he sacrificed and burnt incense in high places." (1 King 3:3 KJV)

Solomon loved the Lord, walking in the statutes of his father David. Solomon offered a thousand burnt offerings in Gibeon and God appeared to him and said to ask, "What shall I give you?" And Solomon asked God to give him wisdom to judge His people and the Lord was pleased with him and God granted his request.

Thus, God is pleased with sacrifices, the way He was pleased with Solomon, and He appeared to him and wanted to give him whatever he asks. When you give offering, pray and fast in secret, that is equal to sacrifice, and the Father in heaven will reward you openly, the way Solomon was rewarded because of his sacrifice.

God the Father is equal to a king, and no one can see or meet the king unless the king wants. The way Queen Esther wanted to meet the king, but she could not. Because, if anyone goes to the king without being called, they can be put to death unless the king holds out a scepter to or have mercy on that person, they can live and meet the king.

If we want to see God and see His salvation, we must also sacrifice. The way in the New Testament, Anna, a prophetess who was eighty-four years old, did not depart from the temple and served God with fasting and prayers, she was able to see the face of Jesus, which is the face of God. And, to another prophet, whose name was Simeon, it was revealed to him by the Holy Spirit that he would not see death before he had seen the Lord's Christ; he was waiting for the consolation of Israel, he saw the face of Jesus.

"And Noah began to be a farmer, and he planted a vineyard. Then he drank of the wine and was drunk, and became uncovered in his tent. And Ham, the father of Canaan, saw the nakedness of his father, and told his two brothers outside." (Genesis 9:20–22)

Noah represents God the Father, and Ham saw His nakedness. *In his tent* means in the holy temple; when we are in the holy temple, we offer ourselves as living sacrifice, destroy the first tabernacle, destroy the sinful works of the flesh, and we enter the second tabernacle, meaning the most holy place where we can see God. So, Noah awoke from his wine and knew what his younger son had done to him, then he said: "Cursed be Canaan; A servant of servants He shall be to his brethren."

Canaan be cursed means die out to the works of the flesh and live according to the Spirit and be a servant of his brethren. The way Jesus said, "The Son of Man did not come to be served, but to serve." Then Jesus washed feet of His disciples.

> And the firstborn said unto the younger, Our father (Lot) is old, and there is not a man in the Earth to come in unto us after the manner of all the Earth: come, let us make our father drink wine, and we will lie with him, that we may preserve the seed of our father. And they made their father drink wine

that night: and the firstborn went in, and lay with her father; and he perceived not when she lay down, nor when she arose. And it came to pass on the morrow, that the firstborn said unto the younger, Behold, I lay yesternight with my father: let us make him drink wine this night also; and go thou in, and lie with him, that we may preserve the seed of our father. And they made their father drink wine that night also: and the younger arose, and lay with him; and he perceived not when she lay down, nor when she arose. Thus were both the daughters of Lot with child by their father. And the firstborn bare a son, and called his name Moab: the same is the father of the Moabites unto this day. And the younger, she also bare a son, and called his name Ben-ammi: the same is the father of the children of Ammon unto this day. (Genesis 19:31–38 KJV)

Lot represents God the Father. The elder daughter said that there is no man on Earth to come into us as is the custom of all the Earth. God is Spirit and He is a Man. The daughters made their father drink wine means they offered their physical body as living sacrifice. *Wine* represents the blood sacrifice. The way Jesus went to the Holy of Holies with His own blood. These daughters, with their sacrifice that was covered by the blood of Jesus and His grace, made God the Father drunk and became one with Him so that they can have spiritual children, spiritual fruits. By doing this, they knew God, they knew how God was. Thus, by knowing God, you can bear the Son. Being one with Him in Spirit, by bearing His Son, you are born again. Newness of life, as Jesus said, "See I make all things new."

The way Lot's daughters knew God the Father, I also knew God. By my sacrifice, fasting, prayer, and offering, I went to the Father, and I saw the Father, knew the Father. I am writing this book about that.

I am married for nineteen years and one night, I had a dream that my husband was lying on the bed in my bedroom without clothes, and I was very happy to see him, and I kissed him all over and my dream ended. In the morning, I thought about that dream and was surprised that I had that dream. But, when I was writing this book, the Holy Spirit revealed the meaning of that dream to me that *husband* means Jesus Christ and he also represents the Father. Because we are a new creation in Jesus Christ, we were all created through Him. We become one with Him, one in the Spirit, and bear holy children means bear holy fruits so that God be glorified. Jesus said, "See I make all things new." New heaven and new Earth, we are a new creation in Christ Jesus. Thus, the Holy Spirit said to me, "You saw the Father as Lot's daughters did."

"The Holy Spirit indicating this, that the way into the Holiest of All was not yet made manifest while the first tabernacle was still standing." (Hebrews 9:8)

So, the first tabernacle is the physical body. If we die related to the works of the flesh, the way into the Holiest of All is open for us and we can see God the Father face-to-face and be one with Him.

72. Asked for a Son

During the time of the judges in Israel, Samuel was judging Israel. The people of Israel asked for a king and this thing displeased Samuel. God said to Samuel, "By asking a king, they have not rejected you, but they have rejected Me." So, God gave them a king according to their request.

King David represents God the Father and God said, "Son of David (Jesus) will reign forever" and thus God gave the son (King).

Abraham was childless, meaning the one who does not bear fruits for God, and he asked for a son. Abraham asked for a son means he asked to be free from sinful flesh and give birth to the son. The Son of promise who will inherit the eternal life.

Rebecca was barren and she asked God for a son and God gave her two sons. Older will serve the younger means the physical will serve the spiritual.

Hanna asked God for a son, "If you will give me a son, then I will give him to the Lord." That son represents Jesus who was offered up for us.

Rachel asked for a son and God gave her a son (Joseph). She had her firstborn son who represents Jesus. He was exalted and the people of the Earth came to buy food from him. He saved the house of Israel from the famine, so they do not perish.

The people of Israel were freed from bondage in Egypt. I called my son out of Egypt. They are the promised sons.

Zacharias and Elizabeth bore a son, John the Baptist in their old age. It was said of him, "I send an angel before Your face, who will prepare Your way before You."

A virgin shall be with child and bear a son. He will become their Savior. Thus, we also give birth to a son. By trusting in His name, we are born again.

In the same manner, the Earth also groans and labors with birth pangs and gives birth to a son which is the new Earth. In the same way, its written about Jerusalem that, "Hagar is Mount Sinai in Arabia, and corresponds to Jerusalem which now is, and is in bondage with her children but the Jerusalem above is free, which is the mother of us all" (Galatians 4:25–26).

This means the people of Jerusalem who are Jewish wanted to be saved by the works of obeying the law through the flesh. But it was impossible to obey the law in all things and, therefore, they are under bondage. The Jerusalem above (Jesus Christ) is free, which is the mother of us all. Every good gift and every perfect gift is from above. Jesus said, "Set your mind on things above and not the things of this world." Those who are obedient to God, abide in Jesus and through Him we are born again. That is the holy city, the New Jerusalem.

"Then one of the seven angels who had the seven bowls filled with the seven last plagues came to me and talked with me, saying, 'Come, I will show you the bride, the Lamb's wife.' And he carried me away in the Spirit to a great and high mountain, and showed me the great city, the holy Jerusalem, descending out of heaven from God." (Revelation 21:9–10)

In Christ Jesus, we are a new creation. The obsolete and growing old is ready to vanish away. Everyone has to be born of the Spirit so that we can be free from the old nature and become new.

73. Journey

"I came forth from the Father and have come into the world. Again, I leave the world and go to the Father." (John 16:28)

Jesus came forth from the Father into this world. From where the first Adam had fallen and lost everything, Jesus came and took everything back for us. The first Adam disobeyed God's commandment, but the second Adam (Jesus) obeyed in all things. Jesus came in the likeness of the sinful flesh and became woman and was tempted as we are tempted. But He did not sin and took all our sins upon Himself and suffered death on the cross and God punished the sin in His body and destroyed sin. The way the physical body is sowed and the spiritual body is raised. On the third day, He rose from the dead. God raised Him through the power of the Holy Spirit, and He appeared to the disciples and talked to them about the kingdom of God for forty days. He was seen by over 500 people and was lifted up in the cloud to the Father and is seated at His right hand. As God said to Jesus to sit at His right hand, till He makes His enemies His footstool. That day is the eighth day means the day of the new heaven and the new Earth. Jesus Christ in His glory will sit on the throne and the son of David will reign forever.

God the Father (Son of Man ascended to Him)
Christ (Raised from the death) (Glorified body)

Man (Jesus) (God's glory)
Woman (Man's glory)

The woman grows her hair and became obedient to the Man (Jesus). By killing her husband of sin, she gives birth to Christ (the way physical is sowed, and the spiritual is raised) and is free from the law. The way Jesus took everything back and was lifted up to the Father, in the same way, we also have to take everything back by becoming a virgin, not having any spot or wrinkle and being married to Christ, becoming one with Him. After rising from the dead, Jesus said to his disciples, "See, for a spirit does not have flesh and bones" the way when woman was created out of Adam, Adam said, " bone of my bones and flesh of my flesh; She shall be called Woman." Therefore, we were created out of Jesus. Thus, woman was created and redeemed by the blood of Jesus.

We came forth from the Father. Like Jesus, we too need to go back to the Father. This way, we become mature. We all went astray but Jesus became the Way and said, "Follow Me." We should follow Jesus as He asked us to. We should follow Him carrying our cross and sacrificing our sinful flesh on the cross and following Him. This is holy and acceptable sacrifice to God.

When Jesus was on the cross, bearing our sins as the enemy sowed tares, we were created out of Jesus that is the woman. So, He took our sins, died, and gave us life.

74. Love of Jesus

"That which has been is what will be, that which is done is what will be done, and there is nothing new under the sun." (Ecclesiastes 1:9)

God told Hosea to take himself a wife of harlotry and children of harlotry because the land has committed great harlotry departing from the Lord.

Hosea represents Jesus and the harlot represents us who disobeyed God and became one with the devil. God asked Jesus to marry us, and Jesus married us. He became one with us. Jesus gave us the commandments and we obeyed those commandments as He said, "Abide in Me, I will abide in you, we become one and bear much fruit for the Father and glorify God." Thus, Jesus became our husband and is one with us, so that by our children (fruits), God be glorified.

Thus, Jesus became one with us. Man will leave his father and mother and be one with his wife. The name *Hosea* means salvation. We are saved by trusting in the name of Jesus.

The name *Samson* means sun. That child shall be a Nazirite to God from the womb. Samson who represents Jesus, in him was lot of strength. He killed 1,000 Philistines. He tore the lion apart as one would have torn apart a young goat. *Lion* represents the devil. The Spirit of the Lord came mightily upon Samson. "And it came to pass afterward, that he loved a woman in the valley of Sorek, whose name was Delilah. And the lords of the Philistines came up unto her, and said unto her, Entice him, and see wherein his great strength lieth, and by what means we may prevail against him, that we may bind him to afflict him: and we will give thee every one of us eleven hundred pieces of silver (Judges 16:4–5 KJV).

The name *Delilah* means delicate. To find out Samson's strength, Delilah tried three times. The fourth time, Samson told her that his strength is in his hair. "He told her all his heart, and said unto her, There hath not come a razor upon mine head; for I have been a Nazarite unto God from my mother's womb: if I be shaven, then my strength will go from me, and I shall become weak, and be like any other man." (Judges 16:17 KJV)

Then Delilah lulled him to sleep on her knees and called for a man and had him shave off the seven locks of his head. *Hair* represents obedience. Jesus was separated for God from His mother's womb. But the woman gave him the fruit of the tree of the knowledge of good and evil and her husband took it and ate and loved the woman. Thus, by taking our sins upon Himself,

He disobeyed God. And the strength of Samson left and then the Philistines took him and put out his eyes. Jesus was made blind, and the God left Him. In Sheol (hell), everyone is naked, exposed, and blind. They cannot see God. And Samson was thrown into prison and, enslaved to sin, became a grinder. Then, the hair of his head began to grow again, and the lords of the Philistines gathered together to offer a great sacrifice to Dagon their god, and to rejoice. And they said that our god has delivered into our hands Samson our enemy!

So, they called for Samson from prison, and he performed for them. And they stationed him between the pillars. Then, by the help of a lad, Samson stood leaning on the pillars that supported the temple. Now, the temple was full of men and women.

Then Samson called to the Lord, saying, "O Lord God, remember me, I pray! Strengthen me, I pray, just this once, O God, that I may with one blow take vengeance on the Philistines for (putting out) my two eyes!" As, at the Mount of Olives, an angel appeared to Jesus from heaven, strengthening Him.

The Temple of Dagon is stated to be a den of thieves that was made by us, which Jesus vowed to destroy and raise up on the third day. Three days to God is 3,000 years, meaning He will raise it up in 3,000 years. Thus, He took revenge for taking His eyes and Samson destroyed that temple. Let me die and Jesus sacrificed His physical body. He sacrificed Himself to save us. Jesus loved us so much that he paid our debt and freed us from the slavery of sin.

75. Yoke

"Come to Me, all you who labor and are heavy laden, and I will give you rest. Take My yoke upon you and learn from Me, for I am gentle and lowly in heart, and you will find rest for your souls. For My yoke is easy and My burden is light." (Matthew 11:28–30)

We are all heavy laden by the works of the law and it's impossible to be justified by them, but we find rest in Jesus. The name *Noah* means rest and Noah, who represents Jesus, built an ark of faith, and few were saved when they were disobedient. So, by trusting in the name of Jesus, we are saved by His hand of grace.

Jesus said, "My yoke is easy, and My burden is light," and John said, "His commandments are not burdensome" (1 John 5:3). Therefore, when we obey God's commandments, which is our love for God, His commandments are not burdensome. So, Jesus' yoke (commandments) is not burdensome.

76. Debt

Sin is debt. This life is given to us by God the Father and, for us, this life is someone else's wealth. If we are not faithful to God for our life and keep gathering the debt of sin, Scriptures say, "If you have not been faithful in what is another man's, who will give you what is your own?" (Luke 16:12).

"Owe no one anything except to love one another, for he who loves another has fulfilled the law" (Romans 13:8). So, we can have the debt of love. Paul says, "We are debtors to Christ because He paid all our debts of sin to God." He suffered death for us. Therefore, there is no condemnation in Christ Jesus, but we have eternal life. We are indebted by his love.

Scriptures say, "You shall lend but you shall not borrow."

77. Rich

And he spake a parable unto them, saying, The ground of a certain rich man brought forth plentifully: and he thought within himself, saying, What shall I do, because I have no room where to bestow my fruits? And he said, This will I do: I will pull down my barns, and build greater; and there will I bestow all my fruits and my goods. And I will say to my soul, Soul, thou hast much goods laid up for many years; take thine ease, eat, drink, and be merry. But God said unto him, Thou fool, this night thy soul shall be required of thee: then whose shall those things be, which thou hast provided? So is he that layeth up treasure for himself, and is not rich toward God. (Luke 12:16–21 KJV)

The rich man's ground yielded plentiful. *Rich man* means rich in sin. The plentiful yield is worldly richness in sin, which is for a short time. The way grass grows today and withers tomorrow, our sinful works do not go with us. Jesus said, "Do not labor for the food which perishes." God said to that rich man, "Fool! this night your soul will be required of you." The sins that were plentiful can be enjoyed only until this physical body lasts. After death, no one can enjoy the pleasure of sin. Therefore, labor for the food that endures to everlasting life.

> There was a certain rich man, which was clothed in purple and fine linen, and fared sumptuously every day: and there was a certain beggar named Lazarus, which was laid at his gate, full of sores, and desiring to be fed with the crumbs which fell from the rich man's table: moreover the dogs came and licked his sores. And it came to pass, that the beggar died, and was carried by the angels into Abraham's bosom: the rich man also died, and was buried; and in hell he lift up his eyes, being in torments, and seeth Abraham afar off, and Lazarus in his bosom. And he cried and said, Father Abraham, have mercy on me, and send Lazarus, that he may dip the tip of his finger in water, and cool my tongue; for I am tormented in this flame. But Abraham said, Son, remember that thou in thy lifetime receivedst thy good things, and likewise Lazarus evil things: but now he is comforted, and thou art tormented. And beside all this, between us and you there is a great gulf fixed: so that they which would pass from hence to you cannot; neither can they pass to us, that would come from thence. Then he said, I pray thee therefore, father, that thou wouldest send him to my father's house: for I have five brethren; that he may testify unto them, lest they also come into this place of torment. Abraham saith unto him, They have Moses and the prophets;

let them hear them. And he said, Nay, father Abraham: but if one went unto them from the dead, they will repent. And he said unto him, If they hear not Moses and the prophets, neither will they be persuaded, though one rose from the dead. (Luke 16:19–31 KJV)

A certain rich man means rich in sin, and he was enjoying sin and fared sumptuously every day. A certain beggar named Lazarus full of sores represents Jesus and those who will be firstfruits with Him. Lazarus was a beggar means he was poor relative to sins. He did not satisfy his flesh. He was fasting and not giving in to sin and not fulfilling the lust of the flesh. As Jesus said, "Whoever seeks to save his life will lose it, and whoever loses his life will preserve it."

As Jesus fasted for forty days, they represent 4,000 years, where He did not sin. Lazarus died and was carried by the angels to Abraham's bosom because he was alive to God. The rich man also died and was buried because he was dead to God. The dead are buried in the field that was bought by the price of the blood of Jesus to bury strangers. The rich man was tormented in Hades because he was separated from God forever.

There was a great gulf between Abraham and the rich man, so that neither those who want to pass from here to there can nor those from there pass to here. This great gulf separates from God forever.

The rich man cried and said, "Father Abraham, have mercy on me, and send Lazarus that he may dip the tip of his finger in water and cool my tongue, for I am tormented in this flame."

The rich man represents Jesus who took our sins upon Himself and ended up at this tormenting place. And Jesus said on the cross "I thirst!" because God had left Him, and He thirsts for life. That living water represents life. Thus, those who are dead according to the works of God will thirst for the living water forever.

And, behold, one came and said unto him, Good Master, what good thing shall I do, that I may have eternal life? And he said unto him, Why callest thou me good? there is none good but one, that is, God: but if thou wilt enter into life, keep the commandments. He saith unto him, Which? Jesus said, Thou shalt do no murder, Thou shalt not commit adultery, Thou shalt not steal, Thou shalt not bear false witness, Honour thy father and thy mother: and, Thou shalt love thy neighbour as thyself. The young man saith unto him, All these things have I kept from my youth up: what lack I yet? Jesus said unto him, If thou wilt be perfect, go and sell that thou hast, and give to the poor, and thou shalt have treasure in heaven: and come and follow me. But when the young man heard that saying, he went away sorrowful: for he had great possessions.

Then said Jesus unto his disciples, Verily I say unto you, That a rich man shall hardly enter into the kingdom of heaven. And again I say unto you, It is easier for a camel to go through the eye of a needle, than for a rich man to enter into the kingdom of God. When his disciples heard it, they were exceedingly amazed, saying, Who then can be saved? But Jesus beheld them, and said unto them, With men this is impossible; but with God all things are possible. (Matthew 19:16–26 KJV)

A young man wanted to be perfect, so Jesus said, "Sell what you have and give to the poor, and you will have treasure in heaven; and follow Me." When the young man heard this, he went away sorrowful, for he had great possessions, meaning the wealth of sin.

Jesus said, "That I am gentle and lowly in heart. Jesus is poor relative to sin. If we give our wealth of sin to Jesus, we will have treasures in heaven."

As Jesus said, "Write to the angel of the church of the Laodiceans, because you say, 'I am rich, have become wealthy, and have need of nothing'—and do not know that you are wretched, miserable, poor, blind, and naked." Which is not rich toward God. "I counsel you to buy from Me gold refined in the fire, that you may be rich; and white garments, that you may be clothed, that the shame of your nakedness may not be revealed; and anoint your eyes with eye salve, that you may see." We should give our wealth of sin to the poor means to Jesus and buy gold refined in the fire and white garments from Him.

Then, Jesus said to His disciples, "Assuredly, I say to you that it is hard for a rich man to enter the kingdom of heaven. And again I say to you, it is easier for a camel to go through the eye of a needle than for a rich man to enter the kingdom of God" (Matthew 19:23–24).

The way to the kingdom of God is narrow and the people of nature as camel can easily enter the kingdom of God. A *camel* is an animal of the desert, and it can stay without food and water for many days. The people with nature as camel are not consumed with sin, and they are fasting by not giving in to sin.

John the Baptist himself was clothed in camel's hair, with a leather *belt* around his waist. John was a prophet. A *prophet* is a friend of God and God shares His heart with the prophet. It's easier for such to enter the kingdom of God.

78. Meaning of Parables

Another parable He spoke to them: "The kingdom of heaven is like leaven, which a woman took and hid in three measures of meal till it was all leavened" (Matthew 13:33).

The kingdom of heaven which a woman took, *woman* represents all of mankind. Three measures mean 3,000 years, and measure of meal represents the body of Jesus and those who are to be firstfruits with Jesus who are the burden carriers and the yoke bearers. The leaven represents sin that was hid in three measures of meal till it was all leavened. The way Jesus took the sins of many.

When the lost sheep is found, the Shepherd calls together his friends and neighbors, saying to them, "Rejoice with me, for I have found my sheep which was lost!" The Son of Man has come to seek and to save that which was lost. The way the father rejoices with his servants when the prodigal son returns. There will be more joy in heaven over one sinner who repents than over ninety-nine just persons who need no repentance.

One woman had ten silver coins and, when she loses one, she lights a lamp, sweeps the house, and searches carefully until she finds it. And, when she has found it, she calls her friends and neighbors to come together, saying, "Rejoice with me, for I have found the piece which I lost!" Likewise, there is joy in the presence of the angels of God over one sinner who repents. This is God the Father's joy!

> Whoever causes one of these little ones who believe in Me to sin, it would be better for him if a millstone were hung around his neck, and he were drowned in the depth of the sea. Woe to the world because of offenses! For offenses must come, but woe to that man by whom the offense comes! If your hand or foot causes you to sin, cut it off and cast it from you. It is better for you to enter into life lame or maimed, rather than having two hands or two feet, to be cast into the everlasting fire. And if your eye causes you to sin, pluck it out and cast it from you. It is better for you to enter into life with one eye, rather than having two eyes, to be cast into hell fire. (Matthew 18:6–9)

There are fewer offenses that come from others. Most of the offenses come from ourselves. As Jesus said, "A man's enemies *will be* those of his own household." *House* represents our body, which is against our spirit and wars against us. Thus, Jesus said, "If your hand or foot causes you to sin, cut it off and cast it from you. It is better for you to enter into life lame or maimed, rather than having two hands or two feet, to be cast into the everlasting fire." Thus, the body (flesh) lusts after sin and, to destroy that, Jesus said, "If you offend your brother, it would be better for you if a millstone were hung around your neck, and you were drowned in the depth of the sea." A *millstone* represents the law. Per the law, a woman caught in adultery was to be stoned to death. This is how hanging a milestone around your neck and to drown in the depth of the sea means to destroy the sins that are in you through the law. Because, through baptism, we bury our body and die to the works of the flesh and live according to the spirit and enter into the newness of life.

The physical body is sown, and the spiritual body is raised. Jesus said, "Every kingdom divided against itself is brought to desolation, and every city or house divided against itself will not stand. If Satan casts out Satan, he is divided against himself. How then will his kingdom stand? Or how can one enter a strong man's house and plunder his goods, unless he first binds the strong man? And then he will plunder his house" (Matthew 12:25–26, 29).

House represents us and *the strong* represents the devil. Our flesh that lusts after sin, we need to bind that in the name of Jesus and, then, we can plunder the house.

Whatever you bind on Earth will be bound in heaven means Jesus, who is the cornerstone, by joining with Him we are built into a temple. Whatever we loose or set free on Earth will be loosed or set free in heaven means you will know the truth and the truth shall set you free. The way we know the truth and that truth sets us free, we will be free in heaven.

79. Woman—Physical Body

"Wives, submit to your own husbands, as to the Lord. For the husband is head of the wife, as also Christ is head of the church; and He is the Savior of the body. Therefore, just as the church is subject to Christ, so let the wives be to their own husbands in everything." (Ephesians 5:22–24)

The way the older will serve the younger is the same way the physical body will serve the spiritual body. *Woman* represents the physical body which should be subject to Christ and obey all His commandments.

When David came to Nob, to Ahimelech the priest, and asked for bread which was not lawful to eat except for the priests, the priest said, "There is no common bread on hand but only holy bread, but they can have it, if the young men have at least kept themselves from women." Then, David answered the priest, and said to him, "Truly, women have been kept from us about three days since I came out."

Thus, *woman* represents the physical body and to be one with her means fulfilling the lust of the flesh.

During the time of Ezra, when the Israelites came back from the captivity of Babylon, they had taken some of their daughters as wives for themselves and their sons, so that the holy seed is mixed with the peoples of those lands.

Thus, we have trespassed against our God, and have taken pagan wives from the peoples of Babylon, yet now there is hope in Israel in spite of this. The Levites had married pagan wives and they made a covenant with God to put away all these wives.

"These sought their listing among those who were registered by genealogy, but it was not found; therefore, they were excluded from the priesthood as defiled." (Nehemiah 7:64)

Genealogy represents the Book of Life. Those who walked according to the flesh, their names were excluded from the Book of Life. Whoever accepts Jesus Christ, their names are written in the Book of Life, and they walk by the Spirit.

The sons of God saw the daughters of men that they were beautiful and they took wives for themselves of all whom they chose and committed adultery. They were beautiful to behold as the fruit of the tree of knowledge of good and evil was pleasant to the eyes. Thus, through the lust of the physical body, they committed sin. To demonstrate this, God has made woman beautiful.

> And Israel abode in Shittim, and the people began to commit whoredom with the daughters of Moab. And they called the

people unto the sacrifices of their gods: and the people did eat, and bowed down to their gods. And Israel joined himself unto Baal-peor: and the anger of the LORD was kindled against Israel. And the LORD said unto Moses, Take all the heads of the people, and hang them up before the LORD against the sun, that the fierce anger of the LORD may be turned away from Israel. And Moses said unto the judges of Israel, Slay ye every one his men that were joined unto Baal-peor.

And, behold, one of the children of Israel came and brought unto his brethren a Midianitish woman in the sight of Moses, and in the sight of all the congregation of the children of Israel, who were weeping before the door of the tabernacle of the congregation. And when Phinehas, the son of Eleazar, the son of Aaron the priest, saw it, he rose up from among the congregation, and took a javelin in his hand; and he went after the man of Israel into the tent, and thrust both of them through, the man of Israel, and the woman through her belly. So the plague was stayed from the children of Israel. And those that died in the plague were twenty and four thousand. (Numbers 25:1–9 KJV)

Whoever lusts after the flesh and were one with the flesh, they were killed and then the plague was stopped among the children of Israel. Those who died in the plague were 24,000. Thus, God does not want mixed people, who get mixed up with sin. God wants people who walk in the Spirit and truth. Scripture says, "Keep yourself from woman. The people who serve in the temple kept themselves from women and if they didn't keep themselves from women, after they bathe, they were considered unclean until evening."

And the Lord God created man of the dust of the ground and breathed into his nostrils the breath of life and man became a living being. God created the physical body from the dust of the ground.

Jesus said to disciples, "Watch and pray, lest you enter into temptation. The spirit indeed is willing, but the flesh is weak"

(Matthew 26:41). Our body is made of the dust of the ground and is weak.

In the times of Noah, "the Lord said, My spirit shall not always strive with man, for that he also is flesh: yet his days shall be an hundred and twenty years" (Genesis 6:3 KJV). We are made of flesh, and we are weak so God will not strive with us forever. All the people of the Earth are woman.

Jesus said, "That which is born of the flesh is flesh, and that which is born of the Spirit is spirit (John 3:6). So, we should walk by the Spirit and do not fulfill the lust of the flesh.

"For he who sows to his flesh will of the flesh reap corruption, but he who sows to the Spirit will of the Spirit reap everlasting life." (Galatians 6:8)

Woman represents the tree of the knowledge of good and evil, and we should not eat that fruit. We should not fulfill the lust of the flesh but walk by the Spirit.

80. Do Not Empower the Devil

One day, before I woke up, the Holy Spirit talked to me and said, "The devil and his demons have surrounded one house so that they can destroy it. I lifted my eyes up and saw that the house belonged to my biological sister, Preeti, was surrounded by the devil and his demons. I saw that they were not doing any movement but only staring at the house to find an opportunity to attack. I asked the Holy Spirit, "What does this mean?" The Holy Spirit said, "As long as you do not give authority to the devil, he cannot do anything to you." Then, the Holy Spirit said, "Do not empower the devil." When the devil came to Jesus, Jesus said, "It is written…" and by proclaiming the Word of God, He didn't give authority to the devil and did not sin.

We must also do the same. If we give authority to the devil, he will be revealed through us. Anger, theft, murder, and such are the works of the devil that are revealed through us. Thus, we should not reveal the devil from within us but reveal Jesus Christ from within us and glorify God.

> And I saw thrones, and they sat on them, and judgment was committed to them. Then I saw the souls of those who had been beheaded for their witness to Jesus and for the Word of God, who had not worshipped the beast or his image, and had not received his mark on their foreheads or on their hands. And they lived and reigned with Christ for a thousand years. But the rest of the dead did not live again until the thousand years were finished. This is the first resurrection. (Revelation 20:4–5)

Those who are dead according to the works of the flesh, they will be part of the first resurrection. They will rule with Christ for 1,000 years during the years 7000s right here on this Earth as Paul had said you reign as kings. This day is God's Sabbath Day in which whoever does the works of the flesh will be cut off from among the people. So, whoever lasts until the end, will be saved.

> Now when the thousand years have expired, Satan will be released from his prison and will go out to deceive the nations which are in the four corners of the Earth, Gog and Magog, to gather them together to battle, whose number is as the sand of the sea. They went up on the breadth of the Earth and surrounded the camp of the saints and the beloved city. And fire came down from God out of heaven and devoured them. The devil, who deceived them, was cast into the lake of fire and brimstone where the beast and the false prophet are. And they will be tormented day and night forever and ever. (Revelation 20:7–10)

When the year 7000 is completed, during the 8000s, those who are dead according to the spirit will be resurrected leading to death right here on this Earth. Thus, the devil will be released from his prison, and they will go out to deceive the nations which are in the four corners of the Earth, Gog and

Magog, to gather them together to battle. They will surround God's beloved city, meaning Jerusalem, where the tree of life is, where God and his saints' camp is. My beloved sister Preeti's house is there as well. In the same way, you yourself are also the beloved city of God. Satan and his angels surrounded that city, and God destroyed them with fire.

Jesus said, "And this is the will of Him who sent Me, that everyone who sees the Son and believes in Him may have everlasting life; and I will raise him up at the last day" (John 6:40). Thus, on the last day during the 8000s (the fourth millennium AD), death will be swallowed up in victory and those who are to be firstfruits with Jesus will be resurrected with Jesus and will sit on His throne with Him. That is Son of David who will reign forever.

81. Second Death

"I call heaven and Earth as witnesses today against you, that I have set before you life and death, blessing and cursing; therefore choose life, that both you and your descendants may live." (Deuteronomy 30:19)

God has given us free will and set before us life and death. God wants us to choose life. *Life* means God the Father Himself and death is sin which is death related to God, being separated from God. Many people of the Earth choose life and many choose death according to their free will.

God the Father is the head. As mind gives command, God the Father has commandments. The people of God have the mind of Christ. God has created the Earth in order and has set limits for everything. The way God has set the boundary for the ocean so that the waters may not pass over and cover the Earth. Therefore, all things stay in order and subjected to God. However, Satan is not a head but a tail and he does not have a mind. He does not have commandments and he is a fool. He creates chaos and brings darkness. He does not have any limit on anything.

The way all fruits and vegetable have their seed in them, all the people of the Earth have God's seed (Christ) in them. Those who accept Jesus Christ, God's seed grows in them and the image of Christ appears in them. But those who reject God say that we do not want you to rule over us and do not want to obey your commandments. "All ungodliness and unrighteousness of men, who suppress the truth in unrighteousness" (Romans 1:18).

Jesus said that I am the way, the truth, and the life, so the truth is Jesus Christ, and the people suppress the truth in unrighteousness and don't let that seed (Christ) be revealed from them and they bring death to that seed. They reject God and remove God from their lives; they say to God that we do not need you. They rebel against God in Whom we live and breathe.

"Hear, O Israel: The Lord our God, the Lord is one!" (Deuteronomy 6:4). The Lord God is one. The heaven is His throne, and the Earth is His footstool. God is a Spirit and the Earth is His soul and the Sprit and soul together are One God.

Scriptures say, "For in Him we live and move and have our being" (Acts 17:28). We live inside of God. Judas Iscariot, who betrayed Jesus, it's written about him that, "Even my own familiar friend in whom I trusted, who ate my bread, has lifted up his heel against me" (Psalm 41:9).

Judas Iscariot represents the multitude of people who reject God and choose death. They bring death to the seed of Jesus Christ by betraying Him and, with the money of betrayal, they buy a potter's field. Now, this man purchased a field with the wages of iniquity; and falling headlong, he burst open in the middle and all his entrails gushed out. And it became known to all those dwelling in Jerusalem; so that field is called in their own language, Akel Dama, that is, Field of Blood.

Thus, this field was bought with the price of the blood of Jesus, in which Gentiles (the dead related to God) are buried.

"And from the days of John the Baptist until now the kingdom of heaven suffers violence, and the violent take it by force" (Matthew 11:12). Thus, by force, they take part of God's kingdom.

The way the rich man ended up in the tormenting place from where he was able to see Abraham and Lazarus, but there was a great gulf between them, which separates man from God for eternity. The rich man represents the multitude of people who reject God. That rich man thirsts for life for eternity but he will not receive that life (God). Fear Him who is able to destroy both soul and body in hell.

82. Esau

When Isaac, the father of Esau, wanted to bless Esau, Jacob deceives his father Isaac and takes all of Esau's blessings. The blessing that was the birthright of the firstborn, Jacob takes that blessing and leaves. Jacob represents us and the firstborn Esau represents Jesus who was the rightful heir to receive all the blessings but, instead, we took all of those blessings. Thus, we received His righteousness, life, and heritance and we gave our death, curse, and sin to Him.

> And Esau said unto his father, Hast thou but one blessing, my father? bless me, even me also, O my father. And Esau lifted up his voice, and wept. And Isaac his father answered and said unto him, Behold, thy dwelling shall be the fatness of the Earth, And of the dew of heaven from above; And by thy sword shalt thou live, and shalt serve thy brother; And it shall come to pass when thou shalt have the dominion, That thou shalt break his yoke from off thy neck. (Genesis 27:38–40 KJV)

You shall break your yoke, meaning dying out to the works of the flesh, then you will be free. Thus, Jesus dies relative to sins on the cross and God raised Him to live according to the Spirit and broke the yoke from His neck.

83. Cain

Cain was the firstborn and Abel was the second born. Cain represents the physical body and Abel represents the spiritual body. Scripture says, "The natural body is first and then the spiritual." Cain killed Abel. The physical (natural) killed the spiritual. Cain said, "It will happen that anyone who finds me will kill me." Therefore, whoever kills Cain, vengeance shall be taken on him sevenfold. That means a physical body is only for 7,000 years and, as the sinful works of the physical body increases sevenfold, we kill, destroy those works, and are purified and become complete. The way the furnace was heated seven times for Shadrach, Meshach, and Abednego, but they were not harmed in anyway. They were promoted by the king.

NINE

FORMS OF JESUS

84. Abel

Abel represents Jesus who had to suffer death for us. The vengeance for killing Jesus was 4,000 years of slavery. And with that whatever wealth of sin we had gathered, it was laid on Jesus to pay. He took burden of all our sins on Himself.

85. Job

Job was a blameless and upright man. The devil took everything from him, and he was struck by painful boils from the sole of his foot to the crown of his head. And he took for himself a potsherd with which to scrape himself while he sat in the midst of the ashes.

"Then Job arose, and rent his mantle, and shaved his head, and fell down upon the ground, and worshipped, and said, Naked came I out of my mother's womb, and naked shall I return thither: the LORD gave, and the LORD hath taken away; blessed be the name of the LORD. In all this Job sinned not, nor charged God foolishly" (Job 1:20–22 KJV). Thus, Job did not sin by his mouth in word.

Job, who represents Jesus, shaved his head, an act representing His disobedience when He ate the forbidden fruit. Job did not sin with his mouth but sinned by works. Jesus took our sins upon Himself. Jesus said to the scribes and Pharisees, "Brood of vipers! How can you, being evil, speak good things? For out of the abundance of the heart the mouth speaks" (Matthew 12:34).

Thus, Jesus didn't sin by mouth but sinned in works. James writes, if anyone does not stumble in word, he is a perfect man that was written for Jesus who didn't sin in word but sinned in works by taking our sins upon Himself.

The devil took everything from Job and, after that, Job argued with his three friends, "I am just, and I did not commit any sin." Job represents Jesus who took our sins upon Himself and suffered death on the cross. These arguments lasted for forty days, meaning for 4,000 years. The end of this 4,000 years represents the eighth day (the fourth millennium AD). On this day, God the Father raised Jesus and those who are to be firstfruits with Him from the dead. And God blessed Job (Jesus) with twice as much as he had before. The way Jacob gave Joseph double inheritance and, in the twelve tribes of Israel, both sons of Joseph received inheritance (Ephraim and Manasseh). The way Elijah said to Elisha, "If you see me going up, you will receive a double portion of the anointing." The way the disciples saw Jesus lifted up in the clouds and Jesus said, "You will do greater works than me (double portion)."

86. Abraham

Abraham, who is the forefather of faith, represents God the Father. The Lord God the Father said to Abraham that I will bless those who bless you means whoever blesses your works of God that are in you, I will bless those. But, whoever curses you means whoever curses my works that are in you to destroy those works, I will curse those.

Therefore, Jesus curses the fig free that represents Jesus' soul. Because Jesus took our sins upon His physical body, He cursed His physical body. Because the evil works of the flesh curse the works of God. Therefore, Jesus cursed His own soul and suffered death on the cross and destroyed sin.

In the Parable of Abraham and Lazarus, Lazarus was sitting in the bosom of Abraham who represents the son who is in the bosom of the father who has seen the father. Besides the son, no one has seen the father. In His bosom means on His thigh; the son sitting on His thigh represents Jesus and those who will be firstfruits with Jesus. *Thigh* represents the promise, and the son is the heir of that promise. The way it was said of the Levites, "But the Levites have no part among you; for the priesthood of the LORD is their inheritance" (Joshua 18:7 KJV).

87. Joseph

Joseph represents Jesus. Joseph was the son of Jacob's old age and he loved Joseph more than all his children. So, Jacob made him a tunic of many colors. The tunic of many colors represents the anointing. There is a rainbow around God's throne. Joseph's brothers sold Joseph because of their jealousy towards him. Joseph was tempted when Potiphar's wife asked him to lie with her day by day, but he didn't sin. The same way Jesus also did not sin. Joseph was thrown into prison even when he was innocent. Jesus was also innocent but, because of our sins, He suffered death on the cross and was in the depth of the Earth for three days and nights. God raised Him up from the dead. The way Joseph was released from prison, exalted, and made equal to Pharaoh, God made Jesus seat at His right hand and made Him equal to God. The same as Joseph, Jesus was exalted above all His brothers. Jesus said, "No one can come to Me unless the Father who sent Me draws him." The same way, people of Earth came to Joseph to buy food.

88. Ruben

"And it came to pass, when Israel dwelt in that land, that Reuben went and lay with Bilhah his father's concubine: and Israel heard it." (Genesis 35:22 KJV)

Jacob said, "Reuben, thou art my firstborn, my might, and the beginning of my strength, The excellency of dignity, and the excellency of power: Unstable as water, thou shalt not excel; Because thou wentest up to thy father's bed; Then defiledst thou it: he went up to my couch. (Genesis 49:3–4 KJV).

Ruben represents Jesus, the firstborn which is the physical body on which Jesus took our sins. Because of our sins, instead of us, Jesus offered up Himself to God as sacrifice. *Sun* represents the Father, the moon, and the mother. The moon also symbolizes the Israelites who get their light from the sun. The moon does not have its own light. Jesus went up to His Father's bed and defiled it means He committed fornication with His mother when Jesus took the sins of the Israelites and the people of the whole world upon Himself on the cross. Jesus took our darkness and gave us His glory. And, by doing this, He became one with us.

89. City of Refuge

> But if he thrust him suddenly without enmity, or have cast upon him any thing without laying of wait, or with any stone, wherewith a man may die, seeing him not, and cast it upon him, that he die, and was not his enemy, neither sought his harm: then the congregation shall judge between the slayer and the revenger of blood according to these judgments: and the congregation shall deliver the slayer out of the hand of the revenger of blood, and the congregation shall restore him to the city of his refuge, whither he was fled: and he shall abide in it unto the death of the high priest, which was anointed with the holy oil. But if the slayer shall at any time come without the border of the city of his refuge, whither he was fled; and the revenger of blood find him without the borders of the

city of his refuge, and the revenger of blood kill the slayer; he shall not be guilty of blood: because he should have remained in the city of his refuge until the death of the high priest: but after the death of the high priest the slayer shall return into the land of his possession. (Numbers 35:22–28 KJV)

City of refuge represents Jesus. We must come to Him and accept Him, so that we don't have to pay for the sins that we committed knowingly and unknowingly. Because He has suffered and was punished for our sins.

The anointed High Priest also represents Jesus. Jesus in the physical body who took our sins upon Himself. We must stay in the city of refuge until the death of the High Priest. The way Jesus suffered death on the cross and destroyed sin, until we die according to the works of the flesh, we must stay in the city of refuge, and we are under the law. But, if the high priest dies, we can return to the land of our possession, meaning we are free from the law. Thus, by following Jesus, we can obtain our salvation.

90. Moses

Moses represents Jesus. When Moses grew up, he went out to see his brethren and looked at their burdens. He refused to be called the son of Pharaoh's daughter, choosing rather to suffer affliction with the people of God. The same way, Jesus left all the glory in heaven and stepped down to Earth for us, to free us from the slavery of sin. Jesus led us in triumph, same as Moses, and led us from slavery to freedom. Jesus loved us and gave Himself for us.

Michael the Archangel, in contending with the devil, when he disputed about the body of Moses, dared not bring against him a reviling accusation, but said, "The Lord rebuke you!" This body represents the dead body of Jesus because God was going to raise Him from the dead. The name *Michael* means a gift from God.

Now, Moses was very humble, more than all men who were on the face of the Earth. Moses represents Jesus. Jesus said, "Learn from Me, for I am gentle and lowly in heart, and you will find rest for your souls" (Matthew 11:29). Jesus obeyed the law fully.

91. Jephthah

> And Jephthah vowed a vow unto the LORD, and said, If thou shalt without fail deliver the children of Ammon into mine hands, then it shall be, that whatsoever cometh forth of the doors of my house to meet me, when I return in peace from the children of Ammon, shall surely be the LORD's, and I will offer it up for a burnt offering.
>
> So Jephthah passed over unto the children of Ammon to fight against them; and the LORD delivered them into his hands. And he smote them from Aroer, even till thou come to Minnith, even twenty cities, and unto the plain of the vineyards, with a very great slaughter. Thus the children of Ammon were subdued before the children of Israel. (Judges 11:30–33 KJV)

Jephthah represents Jesus; when he defeats the people of Ammon and comes home, there was his daughter, coming out to meet him with timbrels and dancing; and she was his only child. This virgin daughter represents us who are born of Jesus. Her as a burnt offering means offering her soul as a living sacrifice. And she proves her love for her father. This one is a chaste virgin, she gives her life for Christ and, by doing this, she proves her love for Christ.

92. Barak

"A prophetess, Deborah said to Barak, 'And against you I will deploy Sisera, the commander of Jabin's army, with his chariots and his multitude at the river Kishon; and I will deliver him into your hand.'"

"And Barak said unto her, If thou wilt go with me, then I will go: but if thou wilt not go with me, then I will not go. And she said, I will surely go with thee: notwithstanding the journey that thou takest shall not be for thine honour; for the LORD shall sell Sisera into the hand of a woman. And Deborah arose, and went with Barak to Kedesh." (Judges 4:8–9 KJV)

When Sisera had fled away from the war to the tent of Jael, the wife of Heber the Kenite. When Sisera was in deep sleep, Jael, Heber's wife, took a tent peg and took a hammer in her hand, and went softly to him and drove the peg into his temple, and it went down into the ground. Thus, God gave a woman glory in killing Sisera.

Likewise, Jesus who became sin, was killed by a woman on the cross. Woman is a weaker vessel but God's strength was revealed through us, weaker vessels and God gave glory to woman.

Woman means those who obey God's commandments and cover their head as a sign of obedience. To destroy the works of the devil, God gave glory to a woman. Jesus' physical body is also a woman who sacrificed His own life. Thus, the devil was killed by a woman.

93. David

"Then it happened one evening that David arose from his bed and walked on the roof of the king's house. And from the roof he saw a woman bathing, and the woman was very beautiful to behold." (2 Samuel 11:2)

"Then David sent messengers, and took her; and she came to him, and he lay with her, for she was cleansed from her impurity; and she returned to her house." (2 Samuel 11:4)

David represents God the Father. David walked on the roof means it represents His status. The way God the Father used to meet Moses on the high mountain. Bathsheba represents the nation of Israel that was cleansed from her impurity.

God the Father first initiated to be one with the people of Israel, so He gave them the law and statutes by which they can be one with God.

And Nathan said to David, "However, because by this deed you have given great occasion to the enemies of the Lord to blaspheme, the child also who is born to you shall surely die." David, therefore, pleaded with God for the child, and David fasted and went in and lay all night on the ground. Then, on the seventh day, it came to pass that the child died. Therefore, David's firstborn (physical body) son died. David pleaded for 7,000 years but the physical body died. Thus, the physical body is only for 7,000 years. David had another son which represents the spiritual body. God named him *Jedidiah*, meaning beloved of YHWH.

And Nathan said to David, thus says the Lord, "Behold, I will raise up adversity against you from your own house; and I will take your wives before your eyes and give them to your neighbor, and he shall lie with your wives in the sight of this sun. For you did it secretly, but I will do this thing before all Israel, before the sun" (2 Samuel 12:11–12).

And Jesus came through the house of David, and He committed adultery on the cross before everyone's eyes. He took the fruit of the knowledge of good and evil from us and ate. He took the darkness of our sins and gave us the light of His glory. He became one with us. He suffered death in our place.

God told David, "Now therefore, the sword shall never depart from your house, because you have despised Me." Thus, Jesus said, "Do not think that I came to bring peace on Earth. I did not come to bring peace but a sword. Then, the war started in us, the sword between the flesh and the spirit as they become contrary to each other.

It was in the heart of David to build a temple for the name of the Lord God, but God said, "You shall not build the temple, but your son who will come from your body, he shall build the temple for My name." David represents God the Father. David, who is from the Old Testament, is a keeper of the law and Jesus, who is the son of David, who is the Son of God, and He is to build the temple. Paul said, "God does not dwell in temples made with hands." But God lives in a living temple. God lives in those who live according to the Spirit. Scripture says, "I am the God of Abraham, Isaac and Jacob, I am a God of the living. So, Jesus died in the flesh, but God raised Him from the dead according to the Spirit. The way Jesus died related to sin and was raised again related to the spirit, the people of the New Testament, who believe in Jesus, by doing the same, will be resurrected with Jesus and sit at the right hand of God.

The people of the Old Testament lived by faith. As the Scriptures say, "The just shall live by faith." They believed the law and lived related to God. The way Enoch walked with God; and, he was not, for God took him. But the people of the New Testament, after the resurrection they become chaste virgins, not having any spot or wrinkle or any such thing, and they will be married to Christ. The people who are alive are the invited guest at the wedding feast and that is their part.

Those who believe in Jesus Christ and are dead to sin, they will rise first with glorious bodies and, after that, those who are alive will convert into the glorious body and shall be caught up together with them in the clouds to meet the Lord in the air. The way through the power of the Holy Spirit, Elijah went up by a whirlwind into heaven on horses of fire; they will go in the same way.

The ones who were first according to the flesh will be last and the last that is spiritual will be first. Jesus said, "Assuredly, I say to you that tax collectors and harlots enter the kingdom of God before you."

"Will the Lord be pleased with thousands of rams, Ten thousand rivers of oil? Shall I give my firstborn for my transgression, The fruit of my body for the sin of my soul?" (Micah 6:7)

God the Father sacrifices His firstborn. *Firstborn* means the physical body which is only for 7,000 years. After that, there will be a new heaven and a new Earth, and all things will become new. Whatever is visible will go away and only the invisible will stay. The physical body will go away and only the spiritual will last.

The transgression of spirit, meaning sin that does not lead to death; if you see your brother sinning that sin, ask God and He will give him life. Destroy the works of the flesh by the Spirit, this is not a sin leading to death.

"Sit at My right hand, Till I make Your enemies Your footstool?" (Hebrews 1:13) This means it's the time until the time fulfills for this physical body for 7,000 years, and the eighth day comes during 8000s, when there will be a new heaven and a new Earth. Then, on the eighth day, Jesus, the son of David, will sit on His Father's throne and every tongue will confess that Jesus Christ is the Lord. And He will reign forever.

Until the bruised reed will not break, and smoking flax will not quench, you sit at my right hand. Until Death is swallowed up in victory, you sit at my right hand means until the 7,000 years are completed, Jesus is to seat at God's right hand.

Those in heaven are those who trusted in Jesus and by the Spirit destroyed the works of the flesh; they will bow their knee at the name of Jesus, by the grace of the Lord Jesus.

Those on Earth who believed in Jesus and are alive, they will bow their knee at the name of Jesus. Those who are from under the Earth, who lived in their sin and didn't accept Jesus, they will also bow their knee at the name of Jesus. Those in heaven, and of those on Earth, and of those under the Earth, will confess that Jesus Christ is Lord.

The way Lazarus was comforted in Abraham's bosom, in the same way those in heaven and those on Earth are. But those from under the Earth are like the rich man who will be in torment. The way, there was a gulf fixed between Lazarus in Abraham's bosom and the rich man; in the same way, they (from under the Earth) will be separated from God forever. That rich man does not have flesh that he can lust after the flesh, but he can see Abraham who represents God and Lazarus who represents Jesus. As the rich man thirsts for a drop of water and asked Abraham to send Lazarus, he will thirst for the water of life. That water of life is Jesus Christ. During their earthly life, they didn't drink the water of life but enjoyed in the lust of the flesh. Therefore, they ended up in this tormenting place. They thirst for that everlasting water of life, but they will not get it because the time was fulfilled.

Jesus means the law because Jesus fulfilled the law. When Moses strikes the rock, which was Jesus, means brings death to Jesus; out of him flows the living water. The Ten Commandments of the law were written on the tablets of stones because of too much eating and drinking and sinning; the hearts of the people had become stubborn and hard. So, God said, "I will take the heart of stone out of your flesh and give you a heart of flesh and no more shall every man teach his neighbor, and every man his brother, saying, 'Know the Lord,' for they all shall know Me." Thus, we are all taught by God.

Jesus said to Peter, "You are Peter, and on this rock, I will build My church." The rock, meaning the law, and on this law which is love, the law is fulfilled in one word, *love*. Jesus came to fulfill the law, so whoever obeys the law is just, and to them Jesus said that whoever believes in me will never die. Jesus is the law so the people of the Old Testament, who had faith in the law, will never die. Blessed are those who are invited to the wedding feast! My just servant will live by the law.

Thus, whoever built his house on the rock is liken a wise man and when the rain descended, the floods came, and the winds blew and beat on that house; and, it did not fall, for it was founded on the rock. The rock means the law and the house is us. If the nation of Israel accepts Jesus as their creator, they will become the bride of Christ, be one with Christ, and reign with Him. Jesus said, "Let the children be filled first, for it is not good to take the children's bread and throw it to the little dogs." Paul said, "Now if their fall is riches for the world, and their failure riches for the Gentiles, how much more their fullness!" Because they are God's chosen people.

94. Solomon

> But king Solomon loved many strange women, together with the daughter of Pharaoh, women of the Moabites, Ammonites, Edomites, Zidonians, and Hittites; of the nations concerning which the LORD said unto the children of Israel, Ye shall not go in to them, neither shall they come in unto you: for surely they will turn away your heart after their gods: Solomon clave unto these in love. And he had seven hundred wives, princesses, and three hundred concubines: and his wives turned away his heart. For it came to pass, when Solomon was old, that his wives turned away his heart after other gods: and his heart was not perfect with the LORD his God, as was the heart of David his father. For Solomon went after Ashtoreth the goddess of the Zidonians, and after Milcom the abomination of the Ammonites. (1 Kings 11:1–5 KJV)

Solomon represents Jesus; the foreign women turn away His heart after their gods. Women represent all the people of Earth. Jesus loved them and took their sins upon Himself, took the forbidden fruit from the woman, and ate. Thus, Jesus worshipped idols.

Solomon in his old age represents maturity through experience in his old age. By this, he (Jesus) fought against the darkness and became mature and did not sin but took our sins upon Himself.

95. Ahab

"And Joshua adjured them at that time, saying, Cursed be the man before the LORD, that riseth up and buildeth this city Jericho: he shall lay the foundation thereof in his firstborn, and in his youngest son shall he set up the gates of it." (Joshua 6:26 KJV)

Jericho represents the physical body. Jesus says this about the Temple of Jerusalem, not one stone shall be left upon another that shall not be thrown down. The physical body (flesh) lusts after sin and perishes so what God has thrown down, no one should build. He is like the one having put his hand to the plow and looks back. Lot's wife looked back behind her, and she became a pillar of salt and perished.

"And Ahab made a grove; and Ahab did more to provoke the LORD God of Israel to anger than all the kings of Israel that were before him. In his days did Hiel the Bethelite build Jericho: he laid the foundation thereof in Abiram his firstborn, and set up the gates thereof in his youngest son Segub, according to the word of the LORD, which he spake by Joshua the son of Nun." (1 Kings 16:33–34 KJV)

Thus, *firstborn* means the physical body and the *youngest son* means the spiritual body, and they both perished.

"And do not fear those who kill the body but cannot kill the soul. But rather fear Him who is able to destroy both soul and body in hell." (Matthew 10:28)

96. Nebuchadnezzar

The tree that thou sawest, which grew, and was strong, whose height reached unto the heaven, and the sight thereof to all the Earth; whose leaves were fair, and the fruit thereof much, and in it was meat for all; under which the beasts of the field dwelt, and upon whose branches the fowls of the heaven had their habitation: it is thou, O king, that art grown and become strong: for thy greatness is grown, and reacheth unto heaven, and thy dominion to the end of the Earth. And whereas the king saw a watcher and an holy one coming down from heaven, and saying, Hew the tree down, and destroy it; yet leave the stump of the roots thereof in the Earth, even with a band of iron and brass, in the tender grass of the field; and let it be wet with the dew of heaven, and let his portion be with the beasts of the field, till seven times pass over him; this is the interpretation, O king, and this is the decree of the most High, which is come upon my lord the king: that they shall drive thee from men, and thy dwelling shall be with the beasts of the field, and they shall make thee to eat grass as oxen, and they shall wet thee with the dew of heaven, and seven times shall pass over thee, till thou know that the most High ruleth in the kingdom of men, and giveth it to whomsoever he will. And whereas they commanded to leave the stump of the tree roots; thy kingdom shall be sure unto thee, after that thou shalt have known that the heavens do rule. (Daniel 4:20–26 KJV)

Nebuchadnezzar had a dream and Daniel interpreted that dream. Daniel said, "The tree that you saw, which grew and became strong, whose height reached to the heavens and which could be seen by all the Earth—that is you O king who have grown and become strong; for your greatness has grown and reaches to the heavens."

King Nebuchadnezzar became proud even when his kingdom and prosperity were from the Lord. All he had was because of the grace of God but he didn't thank God for it; so, he was drove from men and his dwelling was with the beast of the field till seven times pass over. But God did not destroy him but left the stump and roots of his tree, so that when he comes to know that Heaven rules, his kingdom can be assured to him.

Thus, we were proud and didn't thank God when we were under His grace. He gave us life. We rejected Him and spent our lives according to our own will in vain and, for that, God didn't destroy us but drove us out from men till seven times pass over, meaning for 7,000 years He drove us out. After the completion of 7,000 years of Earth, those who humble themselves, they will get their kingdom back.

97. Daniel

"In the first year of Darius the son of Ahasuerus, of the seed of the Medes, which was made king over the realm of the Chaldeans; in the first year of his reign I Daniel understood by books the number of the years, whereof the word of the LORD came to Jeremiah the prophet, that he would accomplish seventy years in the desolations of Jerusalem." (Daniel 9:1–2 KJV)

I understood by the books the number of the years specified by the word of the Lord that He would accomplish seventy years in the desolations of Jerusalem. Seventy years represents 7,000 years. Seventy weeks also represent 7,000 years and one week also represents 7,000 years.

Therefore, after 7,000 years of captivity, we will be free. The eighth day is the day of resurrection. The way Lazarus was raised from the dead on the fourth day. In Fourth Millennium AD, on the day of resurrection, Jesus said, "Loose him, and let him go." Thus, we will be free from our captivity.

98. Tamar

> And it came to pass in the time of her travail, that, behold, twins were in her womb. And it came to pass, when she travailed, that the one put out his hand: and the midwife took and bound upon his hand a scarlet thread, saying, This came out first. And it came to pass, as he drew back his hand, that, behold, his brother came out: and she said, How hast thou broken forth? this breach be upon thee: therefore his name was called Pharez. And afterward came out his brother, that had the scarlet thread upon his hand: and his name was called Zarah. (Genesis 38:27–30 KJV)

The second one who was Pharez came out first. As Jesus said, "The last will be first, and the first last." Thus, the physical body was first but, from now on, the spiritual will be the first. The way Pharez was second but became first, the second Adam is spiritual and will be first.

99. Korah

> Now Korah, the son of Izhar, the son of Kohath, the son of Levi, and Dathan and Abiram, the sons of Eliab, and On, the son of Peleth, sons of Reuben, took men: and they rose up before Moses, with certain of the children of Israel, two hundred and fifty princes of the assembly, famous in the congregation, men of renown: and they gathered themselves together against Moses and against Aaron, and said unto them, Ye take too much upon you, seeing all the congregation are holy, every one of them, and the LORD is among them: wherefore then lift ye up yourselves above the congregation of the LORD? (Numbers 16:1–3 KJV)

Korah and his other brothers rose up against Moses and Aaron because they wanted to serve in the tabernacle of the Lord. But God had only assigned Levites to serve in the temple, so they rebelled against Moses and Aaron. "And the Earth opened her mouth, and swallowed them up, and their houses, and all the men that appertained unto Korah, and all their goods. They, and all that appertained to them, went down alive into the pit, and the Earth closed upon them: and they perished from among the congregation" (Numbers 16:32–33 KJV).

Thus, Korah and his brothers who rebelled against God, represent Jesus, who took our sins upon Himself and rebelled against God and died. So that He can qualify us to serve the Lord. We have received the Spirit of adoption by whom we cry out, "Abba, Father. He has made us priests to His God."

The way no one else can serve in the temple except the Levites, Moses used to meet the Lord on the mountain and, if any animal climbed up, it must be stoned to death, meaning, if any physical body climbs up on the mountain, he must be put to death by the stone which is the law.

But Jesus rebelled against God and with His physical body climbed up on the mountain, He was of the tribe of Judah but climbed up on the temple, and He was killed by the law. Thus, He died to the works of the flesh and God raised Him in the Spirit.

Thus, He made us qualified to serve God.

100. Adam—Beginning of God's Creation

The name *Adam* means "Earth" in the Hebrew language. *Adam* means all the people of Earth who were created out of dirt. Adam is not one but two. The first Adam is the physical body and the second Adam is the spiritual body. God said, "Israel is my firstborn son." All the people of the Old Testament time represent the physical body. When they sinned, God's wrath was poured out on them, and they would die. Jesus (physical body) took our sins upon Himself resulting for Him to drink the cup of God's wrath and He died. Scriptures say that grace and truth came through Jesus Christ (spiritual body). In the New Testament time, the Holy Spirit was given and the rain of grace. First, the physical body and then the spiritual body. First, experience the tree of the knowledge of good and evil and, then, through the spirit new birth. The new heaven and new Earth. He who overcomes will receive a crown of life. Thus, God made man perfect on the sixth day. Thus, God finished all the host of heavens and Earth and Jesus said, "It is finished."

God sacrificed His firstborn (physical body) son to save us. Therefore, the Earth is only for 7,000 years. Scripture says, "I saw in the midst of the seven lampstands One like the Son of Man and His voice was like sound of many waters." That sound is of Jesus and those who are to be firstfruits with Him. The Son of David will reign forever. Amen.

101. God Gave Birth to the Son

"For God so loved the world that He gave His only begotten Son, that whoever believes in Him should not perish but have everlasting life (John 3:16).

God gave birth to His only begotten Son and His name is Jesus Christ.

Then Mary said to the angel, "How can this be, since I do not know a man? And the angel answered and said to her, "The Holy Spirit will come upon you, and the power of the Highest will overshadow you; therefore, also, that Holy One who is to be born will be called the Son of God" (Luke 1:34-35).

Jesus was not born of a man, was not born through a man but born of God. Holy Spirit overshadowed and the Son was born. Holy Spirit led Him to all truth. He walked after the Holy Spirit and didn't commit even one sin. He knew no sin. Whoever is born of God does not sin. If we walk by the Spirit, we will not fulfil the lusts of the flesh. The one born of the Spirit is spirit and the one born of the flesh is flesh.

God gave Abraham His word (promise) that "In your seed all the nations of the earth shall be blessed, because you have obeyed My voice" (Genesis 22:18). That (promise) Word became fresh so that those who walk according to the faith of Abraham are blessed through Jesus Christ. Therefore, God gave sacrifice of His only begotten Son.

"Then the serpent said to the woman, 'You will not surely die. For God knows that in the day you eat of it your eyes will be opened, and you will be like God, knowing good and evil'" (Genesis 3:4,5).

They had relationship with God and God came to visit them daily in the Garden of Eden. They could see God but their eyes were closed related to sin because sin was not yet born and they had not experienced sin. The serpent was their lust of the flesh which talked to them and the woman eats the fruit and also gives to her husband resulting their eyes to be open related to sin and their eyes became blind related to God. And their relationship with God is broken. After that mankind was increased on this earth and sin also increased and every kind of sin ruled over mankind. They conceived sin and gave birth to sin and sin was fully grown. In the book of Revelation, its written about OLD serpent which was the serpent in the Garden of Eden who now was fully grown related to sin and experiencing sin had become mature.

Those who sin keep sinning but God does not sin as He is holy and have never sinned. The way God the Father led Jesus Christ to walk in holiness and raised Him from the dead and gave him birth.

Jesus said I go to the Father and will request Father to send you the Holy Spirit. The way Jesus Christ was born, Holy Spirit also alighted upon us so that by God dwelling in us God would keep us holy. Yahweh would fight for us and we would die related to sin and God would raise us from the dead with Jesus Christ. Thus, God gives us birth.

Scripture says, "Do not call anyone on earth your father; for One is your Father, He who is in heaven" (Matthew 23:9). Because we were born through Him. Through the blood of Jesus Christ, all our sins are forgiven that we committed in the past and we do commit unknowingly in our holy walk. Thus, He who brings good inspiration in us is God. He lives in us and fights against every sin and keeps us holy.

Daniel writes "I watched till thrones were put in place, And the Ancient of Days was seated; His garment was white as snow, And the hair of His head was like pure wool. His throne was a fiery flame, Its wheels a burning fire. A thousand thousands ministered to Him; Ten thousand times ten thousand stood before Him" (Daniel 7). This Ancient of Days is God the Father and His hair was like pure wool that represents maturity in holiness and His garment was white as snow represents His righteousness.

Paul said, if our unrighteousness establishes His righteousness then what can we say? My untruthfulness revealed God's truth and gave Him glory. As many more sins we committed and the darkness become thicker, that's how much more the light increased, and His light shined. He fought with the works of darkness and was victorious. He matured in His holiness.

The way Jesus Christ was raised from the dead related to spirit, in the same way He will raise us up with Him. Jesus Christ was declared to be the Son of God with power according to the Spirit of holiness, by the resurrection from the dead and in the same way, God has given us birth in Christ Jesus. Jesus and those who will be firstfruits with Him to them God the Father says, "You are my son and today I have begotten you" Thus God the Father gave us birth. The son who is in His Father's bosom has seen the Father and besides them, no one has seen the Father.

102. Adam - Son of God

God said to Abraham, "By Myself I have sworn, because you have done this thing, and have not withheld your son, your only son, blessing I will bless you, and multiplying I will multiply your descendants as the stars of the heaven and as the sand which is on the seashore; and your descendants shall possess the gate of their enemies."

The promise (word) God gave to Abraham, John writes about that promise (word) that, "In the beginning was the Word, and the Word was with God, and the Word was God."

The Word means the promise that God gave to Abraham. Word of God represents as seed in the bible. That seed God had kept for us. That mystery of God was kept hidden. That Word (seed) was not yet revealed and God's promise was not yet fulfilled.

The Lord appeared to Abraham by the terebinth trees of Mamre. This appearance represents the things to come in the future. God reveals what will happen in the future by the vision or appearance. And Abraham lift up his eyes and looked, and three men stood by him. These three men that are God the Father, the Son (Word, Seed, Jesus Christ) and the Holy Spirit. The Word (Seed) was with God and the Word was God. Three men represents that God is man which represents spiritual.

When God made Abraham know about the destruction of Sodom and Gomorrah, Abraham made last request to God and said, "Would You also destroy the righteous with the wicked, suppose ten should be found there?" and the Lord said to him, "I will not destroy it for the sake of ten."

The scriptures say, "Then the Lord (Jesus Christ) rained brimstone and fire (Holy Spirit) on Sodom and Gomorrah, from the Lord (God the Father) out of the heavens." Jesus Christ is the only one who can ask the Father for the Holy Spirit for us because we have redemption through His blood.

Lot, being a righteous man, he was tormented in his soul day by day living in Sodom and Gomorrah. To free and redeem Lot, Jesus Christ asks the Father for the fire and brimstone (Holy Spirit) so that He can destroy our sins and rescue us from this wicked world. It was shown here how this promise will be fulfilled in the future.

The earth is woman of the Father and only woman can give birth to children. This is why God formed us out of the earth. Scripture says, "A mist went up from the earth and watered the whole face of the ground and the Lord God formed man of the dust of the ground."

"For You formed my inward parts; You covered me in my mother's womb. When I was made in secret, and skillfully wrought in the lowest parts of the earth. I will praise You for I am fearfully and wonderfully made." (Psalms 139).

God created man out of the ground and that earth represents mother's womb. The way baby is formed in the mother's womb, all the bones are formed and joined together and the whole body is formed, the same way God formed man out of the ground. God created Adam, He is the beginning of God's creation. God breathed into his nostrils the breath of life that is the Holy Spirit and they will call His name "Immanuel" that is God with us. The one born of the spirit is spirit. God gave new birth, created new man. People of Israel have God's word, they are spiritual and the Gentiles are earthly and carnal. God Himself is our peace who made both one. God abolished the middle wall of separation between us and created in Himself a new man from the two. Thus, God created a new man out of the ground. God said, "See I make all things new."

Scripture says that Melchizedek king of Salem brought out bread and wine; he was the priest of God Most High. This Melchizedek is Jesus Christ who brought bread and wine because Abraham walked with God by faith but the blood of Jesus was needed to redeem him for the sins of his past. There is no redemption without the blood of Jesus.

"Jesus said to them, 'Most assuredly, I say to you, before Abraham was, I AM'" (John 8:58).

Because the creation of Jesus (Adam) was through the womb of the earth (woman). Scripture says, ""Before I formed you in the womb I knew you; Before you were born I sanctified you" (Jeremiah 1:5). Every male who opens the womb shall be called holy to the Lord.

Therefore, Jesus Christ is the firstborn who opened the womb of the earth and came out. He is the firstborn. Jesus Christ declared to be the Son of God with power according to the Spirit of holiness, by the resurrection from the dead" (Romans 1:4). Adam the Son of God. "I will declare the decree: The Lord has said to Me, 'You are My Son, Today I have begotten You" (Psalms 2:7).

Jesus Christ was seen by more than five hundred people and when He was taken up, a cloud received Him out of their sight. No one has ascended to heaven besides Him. Jesus Christ was born first, and we were all born through Him. Scriptures say, " For by Him all things were created that are in heaven and that are on earth and all things were made through Him, and without Him nothing was made that was made." God gave us new birth through Jesus Christ.

Therefore, all who walk according to the faith of Abraham, they all receive new birth in Jesus Christ. Abraham was also born through Him. This earth is for 7000 years. All people of the earth who have faith as Abraham are all new creation in Christ Jesus. See new heaven and new earth, the old has passed away.

When we were dead in trespasses, God made us alive together with Christ (by grace you have been saved), and raised us up together, and made us sit together in the heavenly places in Christ Jesus. Thus, the promise that God gave to Abraham was fulfilled through Jesus Christ and we have the hope of resurrection in Christ Jesus.

"For as Jonah was three days and three nights in the belly of the great fish, so will the Son of Man be three days and three nights in the heart of the earth" (Matthew 12:40). Three days and three nights represent 3000 years. We were created in the womb of the earth in Christ Jesus. Jonah prayed from the belly of the fish and God answered him.

Jesus Christ is forever. The way the son of man was lifted up. The face of Jesus on the cross is the face of God. God is dead related to sin. He is holy and does not sin. Jesus Christ is revealed through those who are crucified to this world in Christ Jesus and through them Jesus makes intercessory prayers. The Spirit Himself makes intercession for us with groanings which cannot be uttered.

Those who are crucified in Christ Jesus, their face is like the face of God. The way Paul says, we have the mind of Christ. The way brain gives command, they are the angel of the church, they are the kings of this earth.

On the last day, they will be firstfruits with Jesus Christ and the son of David will reign forever! Amen.

103. Gentile (Adulterous Woman)

"He (Jesus) answered and said, 'I was not sent except to the lost sheep of the house of Israel" (Matthew 15:24).

God had given promise (word) to Abraham for his descendants, so Jesus Christ said that I was not sent except to the lost sheep of Israel. But the Israelites, the elders, the Pharisees, and scribes rejected Jesus Christ.

"Jesus said to them, 'Have you never read in the Scriptures: 'The stone which the builders rejected has become the chief cornerstone. This was the Lord's doing, and it is marvelous in our eyes?'" (Matthew 21:42).

Jesus Christ is the Word that was given to Abraham but Israelites rejected Him and delivered him over to the Gentiles to crucify Him.

When the Lord began to speak by Hosea, the Lord said to Hosea: "Go, take yourself a wife of harlotry and children of harlotry, for the land has committed great harlotry by departing from the Lord." Hosea represents Jesus Christ and the harlot represents Gentiles (woman). Hosea went and took Gomer the daughter of Diblaim as wife, and she conceived and bore him a son named Jezreel and she bore a daughter and named her Lo-Ruhamah, for God will no longer have mercy on the house of Israel, but will utterly take them away. After that she bore a son and named him Lo-Ammi, for you are not My people, and I will not be your God.

So God says to Israel that it shall come to pass in the place where it was said to them, 'You are not My people,' There it shall be said to them, 'You are sons of the living God'.

When Jewish people delivered Jesus (husband of sin) to Gentiles, the Gentiles crucified Him and accepted the word of God. Israelites who are people of God, they are spiritual and represent as man and the Gentiles represent as woman.

When Deborah was a prophet, she said to Barak that God will deliver Sisera, the commander of Jabin's army unto his hands. But Barak said to Deborah that if you will go with me then I will go and if not, I will not go. So Deborah said to Barak, "I will surely go with you but there be no glory for you, for the Lord will sell Sisera into the hands of a woman." Then Jael, the wife of Heber, the Kenite woman took a tent peg and drove the peg in to Sisera's temple and killed him.

Barak represents Israel and the woman represents Gentiles. When Jesus was delivered to Gentiles, they crucified Him and killed the husband of sin and woman received the glory.

Jesus said, "Assuredly, I say to you that tax collectors and harlots enter the kingdom of God before you" (Matthew 21:31). So the Gentiles will enter the kingdom of God and the last will be first and the first will be last.

Thus, the Word was delivered to Gentiles by Israelites so that all the nations of the earth would be blessed through the promise that was given to Abraham.

TEN

DREAMS

104. God's Kingdom Inside of Me (Sejal)

About eighteen-and-a-half years ago, our church members got together and prayed in tongues. A sister named Archana Amin translated my tongues into: "God is saying that I will take away your heart full of darkness and will give you a heart full of light." After that, one afternoon, I was taking a nap with my two sons and the Holy Spirit took me in the spirit to show me some things outside. When I came back to my house, I saw a thing full of light equal to a fistful. A bright glorious light was coming out of that thing and my younger son Yeshua's feet were toward that thing. When I return to my body, I saw that my son's feet were toward my heart, where I saw that glorious thing full of light, and I realized that it was my heart that God has made full of light.

During these days, the Holy Spirit said, "Didn't I say to you that God's kingdom will come inside of you?"

God's Kingdom is full of light, and you can see God. With God, there is no variation or shadow of turning, because God is full of light. God is faithful and He has fulfilled all the dreams and visions that He has given me.

105. Samson Tore the Lion Apart Dream

One night, I had a dream that my husband and I were standing in front of the den of lions, and I had a small hand knife in my hand. The lion came to me from the jungle, and I cut his throat with a hand knife and killed him. My husband started a fire there and roasted the meat of the lion. After that, two more lions came to me and I also cut their throat and killed them with the hand knife; then, my dream ended.

Recently, the Holy Spirit explained this dream to me, "The way Samson tore the lion apart; this lion represents the devil and, after some time, when he returned, he turned aside to see the carcass of the lion and found honey in the carcass. This honey represents the revelation of God. In the same way, you killed the lion with a hand knife, the knife represents the Word of God and you have received this book as revelation of God."

106. Daniel's Den of Lions Dream

One night, my husband had a dream. He told me there were three big lions in our house and, when he saw them, he hid himself. I was drying clothes on a rack inside the house as we dried them inside the house during rainy season. My husband tried to warn me about the three lions in the house by so many hand signs, but I had no attention to them. Those lions were walking around me, but they didn't harm me; then, my husband's dream ended. When my husband shared this dream to me, the Holy Spirit explained the meaning of the dream, "The way Daniel was in the lion's den and they couldn't devour him, the lions could not devour you. Lion represents the devil, and he could not devour you because the devil walks about like a roaring lion, seeking whom he may devour; but, if our bodies do not fulfill the lust of the flesh, the devil cannot devour us. God stops the mouth of lions."

107. Heaven on Earth

The book that God asked me to write, He asked me to name it *"Heaven on Earth."* I asked God to confirm to me if the name of the book should be *"Heaven on Earth."* So, God reminded me a dream and, in that dream, Jesus and I were walking around in heaven holding hands. Jesus put a golden bracelet on my wrist, and I got very excited. We were sitting on a ladder that can reach from Earth to heaven and we were talking with each other. The ladder was a white ladder. We were sitting on the ladder and were hanging our feet downwards. From behind us, God the Father came, and He said, "Do not turn around and see as I am coming down on the Earth." When God the Father came closer on the ladder, I saw a great light and my dream ended. God reminded me of this dream and said, "I want to be revealed in you, revealed on this Earth."

I am Earth and God the Father is heaven. The way God lived inside of Adam and Eve in the Garden of Eden, which means a pleasant place. When the voice came out of the clouds, Jesus said the voice didn't come for me but for you. "I have both glorified it and will glorify it again." The way God used to live with us before in the Garden of Eden, He will live with us again. Jesus answered and said to Him, "If anyone loves Me, he will keep My word; and My Father will love him, and We will come to him and make Our home with him" (John 14:23). God's tabernacle with man and, by doing this, God is revealed inside of me on this Earth through this book. Heaven is coming down on Earth and God will reign for 1,000 years. God's Sabbath Day is during the years 7000s .

108. Pregnancy Dream

One night, I had a dream that I was nine months pregnant and my time was completed. I went to the doctor for my check-up and the doctor said that there is little time left. I went to the garden in the middle of the hospital to walk. I saw that I was holding someone's hand and that was my son. When I saw closely, it was my firstborn son Binyamin. My son is eighteen years old, and his face was glorious. He looked at me and gave me a beautiful smile. After that, my dream ended.

Son represents Jesus. As Scriptures say, "She (woman) will be saved in childbearing if they continue in faith, love, and holiness, with self-control" (1 Timothy 2:15). Thus, by conceiving faith and continuing in love, holiness, and self-control, we should bear Christ (Divine Son).

The way Sarah had a son, and she named him Isaac. The name *Isaac* means laughter. Sarah said that God has made me laugh and all who hear will laugh with me. In the same way, God has also given me a son and made me laugh.

109. Husband's House

One night, I had a dream that I was in my husband's house and that house was very dusty and had a lot of trash. Then, I saw my husband from his back. He was extremely tired after working hard that his T-shirt was soaked with sweat. I told him, "Go in the bedroom and rest and I will clean up your whole house for you." My husband went to the bedroom to rest and, after that, I cleaned the whole house. I cleaned all the dishes and pots in the house one by one and cleaned all things. The whole house and all the things in it started shining. Then, my dream ended.

Husband represents Jesus and *house* represents the temple. God the Father has called me to clean his house to prepare a chaste virgin, without spot or wrinkle and without blemish, to present to Christ.

110. Mirror Dream

When I started writing this book, I had a dream and I saw a big mirror. I was standing in front of it and my friend Christine Crowder was with me. After that, I held Christine's hand and went inside of the mirror and inside was another mirror. I also went in that mirror with Christine. My dream ended there. *Mirror* means the Word of God. We can see the Word of God from outside but, through this book, we can see the Word of God from inside. When I was writing this book, my friend Christine called me. I shared my dream with her, and she said to me, "Going into the mirror seems like going behind a curtain." The first curtain is holy place, and the second curtain is the most holy place where God is. I told her that through this book we will be able to see God face-to-face and see how beautiful He is. The way Moses was talking to God face-to-face, we will also be able to see God face-to-face. Amen.

About the Author

Sejal Macwan, the daughter of Vatsala Christian and Pramodrai Clark, was born in a small town called Borsad in the Kheda district, State of Gujarat, in India and raised in Baroda, Gujarat, India. Sejal studied to be a nurse practitioner and worked as a nurse for a few years. Sejal is married for twenty years to her husband Ashishkumar Macwan. Sejal was a full-time mother after the birth of their three children: Binyamin, Yeshua, and Isha. Ever since she received Jesus Christ as her Lord and Savior, she decided to love Jesus to the fullest extent by looking up all commandments and being obedient to Him. Her journey was difficult, but she kept pushing forward. God was with her and was gracious to her in the journey to bring her this far. In 2021, she was blessed to receive many Bible Scripture revelations directly from God. She wrote her first book, *Heaven on Earth*, in 2021, which was then published in 2022.

The revelations in this book are mind-blowing and so amazing that God's handprint is all over it. God is so gracious to all of mankind to give such revelations to truly understand who God is and what His plan is for all of us.

All the glory to God the Father and His Son Jesus Christ. Amen.

www.ingramcontent.com/pod-product-compliance
Lightning Source LLC
Chambersburg PA
CBHW071438150426
43191CB00008B/1168